ACHARYA USTAD ALLAUDDIN KHAN

MUSICIAN FOR THE SOUL

T0049174

ANJANA ROY

Rev. date: 09/19/2013

To order additional copies of this book, contact:
Xlibris LLC
1-888-795-4274
www.Xlibris.com
Orders@Xlibris.com
61932

Contents

Acknowledgments 7
Introduction 11

Chapter 1: Ancestry and Early Period 15
Chapter 2: With Gurus (Teachers) 26
Chapter 3: Mastery in Different Instruments 46
Chapter 4: System of Teaching 53
Chapter 5: Vast Achievements 93
Chapter 6: The Master's Recordings 118
Chapter 7: Baba's Disciples 120
Chapter 8: In His Illustrious Grandson Ustad Ashish Khan's Words 134
Chapter 9: Conclusion 136

Bibliography
Part I 143

Appendices
Appendix I: Letters 149
Appendix II: Ali Akbar Khan's Assessment 153

Dedicated to my parents

Shrimati Swarnalata Devi and Shri Rebati Ranjan Debnath.

Acknowledgments

THE GREATEST INSPIRATION for me for this presentation and my guide for this work was my father, the late Shri Rebati Ranjan Debnath, one of the senior disciples of Ustad Allauddin Khan. My father's constant care for and interest in my research work was instrumental in putting through the material in this book.

As well, my immense gratitude goes to Shri Ganendra Chandra Dhar who helped me and led me in every possible way for the completion of my project. I take great pleasure in expressing my heartfelt thanks and indebtedness to Ustad Ali Akbar Khan, Shri Ashish Khan, Pandit Ravi Shankar, Shrimati Sharan Rani, Pandit Vinay Chandra Maudgalya and Shrimati Sumati Mutatkar who helped me by allowing me to have conversations with them that enlightened me on many an intricate point relevant to my subject. I am also deeply thankful to my teacher and mentor, Pandit Debu Chaudhuri, Dean of music faculty, Delhi University (1981).

I must also express my gratitude to the authors whose works provided me with much food for thought. Their names have been mentioned in the main text as well as in the Bibliography. I thank lavishly the librarians of the faculty library of Sangeet Natak Academy library and its staff.

My deepest thanks goes to my son Subrato Roy for his untiring help, patience and support in the completion of my project. I express great gratitude to my long time friend, co-musician and guide Anand Patole, without whom I could not have even thought of putting my dissertation in the form of a book. I am immensely grateful for the emotional support of Michael Guida, a versatile and master musician, and deeply appreciate his belief in my project. I give special thanks as well to Sarwar B. Salam for offering his help in the completion of this work.

Among others who sparked my thinking and who helped me in different ways for the completion of this project, my deep thanks goes to Valerie Denner and Nirmala Gopinath who helped me immensely in transcribing the previously written transcripts of my dissertation. It was imperative to the publication of this book. Valerie Denner's technical expertise was paramount to getting the original dissertation into the first stage of realizing the work into book form. I also appreciate Valerie for all the encouragement she has given me to enhance my musical career.

I am very grateful to Prasanna Singh, who has inspired me with his musical expertise. From the bottom of my heart, I thank Francine Locascio, Phil Neri, Deepak Jain, Deepankar Maitra, and my good friend and excellent musician Eric Alabaster and his wife Kathy Levine; they have all helped me in many important ways. I am very fortunate to have received musical guidance from the excellent sitarist Shri Parimal M Sadaphal from Delhi, who is one of the foremost disciples of Pandit Ravi Shankar.

I am grateful to Aniruddh Vasant Rai for helping me set up the genealogical tree-chart and providing me with valuable information regarding his illustrious father Pandit Vasant Rai, master sarodist and senior disciple of Ustad Allauddin Khan.

I offer my sincere gratitude to Polash Gomes, the wonderful tabla player and the founder and director of Rageshree Music Institute in New York. I give special thanks to Purneema Desai, the founder and director of Shikshayatan Cultural Center in New York.

My deep appreciation goes to Jagjit Singh, a musician of great caliber, the superb violinist Michael Braudy, the fine sitarist Daisy Paradis, and Ranjan Nandi, an upcoming and highly talented tabla player for keeping me engaged in the world of music.

I am very thankful to Sanjay Sharma, the head of Rikhi Ram (musical instrument makers), who is also the grandson of the late Pandit Rikhi Ram (the founder of the renowned establishment), for providing me with valuable information and helping me with the maintenance of my sitar.

I give special thanks to Siddharth Mehta for his great help in the designing of the book, including the excellent cover. Without his help, I would not have been able to finish my book.

In addition also my deepest gratitude goes to my close friends and family members without whose support I would not have been able to complete this work. They are: Asim Roy, Ranjana Meera Thomas and Robert Harish Thomas, Somesh and Sheila Debnath, Sitesh and Rita Debnath, Chandana and Shantanu Muhuri, Patricia Kharag Prema, Susan Overko and Sharmistha Choudhury. And among them, I cannot but help thank Prodosh Nath, a family friend and great scholar for encouraging me on during the journey of wrting this book.

I offer my heartfelt thanks to Misha Masud, a fine musician and a close friend, for providing the unique and precious pictures of Ustad Allauddin Khan, which helped me immensely to complete this book.

I am truly honored and deeply touched to have Mary Khan's contribution for the enhancement of this book.

Lastly, my sincere thanks goes to my superb editor Shri Amitabh Chattopadhyay. It was a great pleasure to work with him. Without his guidance and direction my dream of publishing this work would not have come true.

Shri Rebati Ranjan Debnath

Senior Disciple of Ustad Allauddin Khan

MY FATHER, THE late Shri Rebati Ranjan Debnath, was a man of the noblest character and stellar talent, and was one who reached rare levels of accomplishment in all areas of life. A great musician and a scholar of the highest erudition, he was known for his honesty and iron will. He believed that relentless persistence attains a goal more completely than haste, and his kind-hearted and hard working nature was known to all close to him. A disciple of Ustad Allauddin Khan – and a "disciple" in every sense of the word – my father was considered *Dharma Putra* (son by virtue) by the master, and he followed his guru's (teacher's) footsteps in his attitude and approach towards life. Like his guru, Shri Debnath believed that when someone helps you with a glass of water, in return one should offer a glass of honey. Although my father did not become a star in the field of Indian classical music, he received immense affection and blessings from his father-like guru which gave him protection throughout his life. Even after a full days worth of work, he would spend countless hours sharing with his children, or any other person who was interested, his immense knowledge of Hindu philosophy, music or the Sanskrit and English languages. He was tireless in giving and sharing to others whatever he had, very much like his guru and father-like figure Shri Allauddin Khan.

Shri Rebati Ranjan Debnath was also a great scholar of the Shrimad Bhagavad Geeta (the holiest book of the Hindus), and plumbed the depths of this universally revered book which addresses every aspect of life in the most illuminating ways He could go on expounding upon the meanings of the shlokas (verses) of the Geeta strictly from memory.

Like his guru, Shri Debnath was a firm believer in rejecting any idleness in life. He did not like wasting any moment. Since my father considered Ustad Allauddin Khan the same as his father, we children addressed the great master as Dadu (grandpa). We called Ustad Ali Akbar Khan (Allauddin Khan's illustrious son) Kaku (paternal uncle) and Shrimati Annapurna Devi (virtuoso daughter of Allauddin Khan) as Pishima (paternal aunt). Upon the passing of his guru, my father observed the religious rites as a son would. My mother, the late Shrimati Swarnalata Devi, was the driving force behind my father, and supported him in every possible way.

Shri Rebati Ranjan Debnath 6th from left with Tanpura

Shri Rebati Ranjan Debnath

Introduction

IN EVERY AREA of endeavor and in every culture, certain personalities appear from time to time that profoundly affect the course of a particular field for generations to come. In the sphere of North Indian Classical Music, historical figures such as Swami Haridas, Mian Tansen, Sadarang, Masit Khan, Bhatkhande and such persons of import come to mind. Each such person affects the art, or a particular aspect of the art, in such a way that they shape the very standards of excellence, and even the requisite repertoire, which would have to be adhered to by future practitioners. What they contribute becomes a part of the lexicon and required knowledge for the serious professionals in the field.

North Indian Classical Music is a type of music that covers a range of expression and depth impossible to fathom. It is not folk music, although like all advanced music, the folk elements play an essential part in the material. Nevertheless, Hindusthani (North Indian) Classical music is one of the most academically difficult musics to master. Thus, the contributions made by the aforementioned luminaries must be considered to be of the most elevated kinds on a world-scale, whether in the arts or sciences (as without the scientific elements of this music, so thoroughly explored and required by the classical practitioners of this art in North India, the expected artistic expression would not even be possible).

In the 20th Century, India was fortunate to have another such musical pioneer, the great Ustad (maestro) Allauddin Khan, create new pathways in musical culture. He broke the bonds of orthodoxy and closed-mindedness of the old families and teaching lineages who held the wisdom of the Raga and Tala music of North India and brought it out to the modern world, without sacrificing the integrity of the art in any way whatsoever. Allauddin Khan's achievements as a performer was historic in itself – one who would be remembered as one of the greatest virtuosos and musical thinkers of all time. And at the same time, his service to India and the world in bringing this ancient art out of exclusivity and make it available for all who are sincerely interested (listeners and performers) is perhaps an achievement on the scale of the great social reformers to whom we owe verily the progressive quality of our daily lives today.

Without Ustad Allauddin Khan's arduous efforts to first plumb the depths of the vast ocean of Indian Music and then setting an example as both an unparalleled musician and a noble-hearted man, it is highly possible that the efforts by such progressive-minded music scholars as Bhatkhande, Paluskar, Ratanjankar and such others would still be hindered by the crippling conservatism that had neither preserved the music in its pure form nor allowed it to naturally progress by incorporating new ideas that enhanced the art. It is not an exaggeration to say that Allauddin Khan's work was a seed for the eventual ambassadorial role that North Indian (and for that matter South Indian) Classical music would take up, representing Indian Culture to the world for decades to come.

Thoroughly versed in the soundest traditional aspects, the Ustad made innovations for the betterment of the art, in presentation, teaching and instrumental improvements based on those very same time-tested traditional principles. Among those who took Indian Music out to the world, his many illustrious students counted the largest in number, both in performance and teaching. This is not because his line of playing was superior to other lines, nor did he or would he ever have claimed such a thing (as it was not part of his perspective whatsoever,) but his very nature compelled him to not withhold what he had gained as far as musical wisdom from anyone who showed promise, had talent and was sincere. This type of thinking was, and to a great degree still is, missing from most lines of North Indian Classical Music. Much of the teaching of this music from old and venerable lines is still held within insecurely-minded families and bound by back-biting politics. This fact is not a matter of opinion. It is known by anyone who even wishes to find out. Even today, there are very few places where one can go to get the real teaching of North Indian music without either being subject endlessly to elementary musical academics (such as the rudimentary versions taught in most institutions – which cannot make one a professional musician in the end), or incorrect information about the Ragas. This incomplete training usually has a high monetary price, and if the training is private (one to one) it usually includes subservience to some family or teacher.

In the field of North Indian Classical Music and as well in his personal life, Ustad Allauddin Khan was a bridge between the good that is in tradition and the the good in the open thinking of modern times. Believing in the direct and one to one teaching between teacher and student (although he taught for ensembles as well), he tirelessly worked to spread the wisdom of this art, both as a performer of legendary status and a landmark educator. Some even put him on the level of a "musical reformer" – much the same as a "religious reformer" or "social reformer" – one who distills the beneficial wisdom from the useless and dogmatic mire and makes it fit for the betterment of the (musical) experience in the present day.

It is impossible to sketch a life-portrait of a man of such scope, particularly as Ustad Allauddin Khan's achievements spanned close to a hundred years. He lived over a century and continued his work until his very last days. This book has endeavored to give the reader a glimpse of his extraordinary life, as an artist, as a historically significant contributor to this great art, and as a man of noble character. It is hoped that the reader will take into consideration the limitations of a book and of language itself, as it is not possible to convey the experience of the Ustad's performance, the effects of his teaching or his presence. But perhaps words can act as a reflection of the great man's life and work and spark within the reader a bit of what was felt by those who were around him. This work is humbly offered to his memory and legacy.

Amitabh Chattopadhyay

Chapter I

ANCESTRY AND EARLY PERIOD

ANCESTRY

ALLAUDDIN KHAN WAS born in Shibpur, a village in the district of Tripura, now in Bangladesh and renamed as the Comilla district. The exact year of his birth is uncertain, although there is evidence that points to an exact year. That will be covered in the course of this first chapter, as it will be proper to throw some light on his ancestral home and forefathers before addressing the early years of the master's life.

Some two hundred years ago, Tripura was a sprawling mountainous region, filled with dense forests inhabited by several tribes, which still remained at a stage of uncivilized barbarism. Some among them were thought even to indulge in cannibal habits. Because of the great difficulty of communication and the wildness of the habitat there was no contact between these tribes and the outside world. It has been surmised that these peoples could not even use fire, and that they fed on raw flesh, sometimes even human.

In this environment, in a cave in the hills, it seems that there was a temple, or a shrine, dedicated to the Goddess Kali, where an idol of Her likeness was worshiped. The priest who looked after the idol was a *tantrik* (a devotee following the cult of *tantra*) named Dinanath Deb Sharma. All of his time was spent in penance of the most difficult sort in the pursuit of *tantrik sadhana*. A number of his disciples lived in distant villages. He had also been able to command considerable respect from the tribal peoples who viewed him and his tantrik ways with a kind of awe and even a certain amount of fear. No one knew how Dinanath had come to be associated with the temple or the place. Many – including the tribes in vicinity – thought that by means of his supernatural powers, Dinanath had been protected from both mundane sufferings as well as torture and death at the hands of the primitive jungle inhabitants. Whether this was true or not, one thing about Dinanath was certain: he had led a family life before taking up residence in the forest.

Prior to moving to the unapproachable hills and jungles, Dinanath had married and had fathered a son. His wife expired shortly after the birth of the child, and the responsibility of bringing up the boy rested entirely upon Dinanath's shoulders. For seven long years, he did whatever was in his power to bring up his child in a proper manner. All along however, he had been burning inside with the desire to leave worldly life and go out in search of lofty spiritual attainments.

Dinanath's child, Shiraju, was handsome and intelligent. From his childhood, Shiraju endeared himself to many by his great zeal for rendering service to others. He made no distinction of caste, creed, status or wealth in giving his voluntary service. Following this approach to life eventually let him to join group led by Debi Chowdhurani. This great woman was a political revolutionary of widespread repute and her associates were known for their social activism, based on a philosophy of equitable economic distribution for all.

However, the British Government, which ruled India at that time, had put out a warrant for the arrest of Shiraju, with the offer of a reward for anyone who would be able to hand him over to the police. In order to protect himself, Shiraju changed his religion and became a Mohammedan (Muslim), taking the name of Samas Fakir. He moved about unrecognized under the cover of his new identity. Within a few years, he reintegrated into a stable and peaceful domestic life, marrying a young Bengali Muslim girl and settling down at his ancestral place in Mulagram, a village near Shibpur. This village was in the Brahmanbaria sub-division of Tripura and was adjacent to the Hill Tippearh district, which at present is the Indian State of Tripura.

Samas Fakir and his wife had two sons, Azhar Mohammad and Chhali Mohammad. Azhar, in his turn, left three sons, namely, Ali Mohammad, Sali Mohammad and Jaffar Mohammad. Ali Mohammad's son was Madar Hussain. Safdar Hussain was Madar Hussain's son and was nicknamed as Sadhu Khan. Five sons and two daughters were born to Sadhu Khan. They were Samiruddin Khan, Aftabuddin Khan, Madhumalati Khatoon, Allauddin Khan, Kedar Khatoon, Nayab Ali Khan and Ayet Ali Khan. Thus, Sadhu Khan and his wife Harasundari Khatoon were the parents of the future musical giant, Ustad Allauddin Khan.

Sadhu Khan, as his name indicates, was a man of kind and generous heart. ("Sadhu" – "sage" or "sagacious") He was deeply fond of, and had a great attachment for, music. Allauddin's mother, Harasundari Khatoon, was a woman of strong character and strict discipline. It seems that the child Allauddin inherited his musical mind and affinity for all things musical from his father and a keen predilection for precision as well as a strong sense of good behavior and decorum from his mother. Here it may be appropriate to cite the genealogy of the great maestro, which is as follows:

GENEALOGICAL CHART OF USTAD ALLAUDDIN KHAN

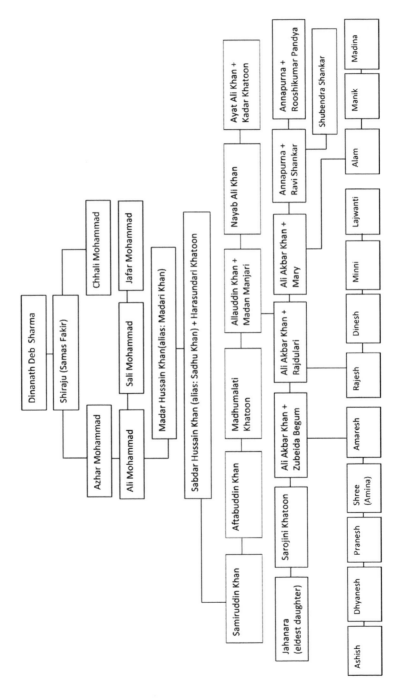

*   Author's note: at the time of the writing of this work, the great master sarodist Ustad Ali Akbar Khan, son of Ustad Allauddin Khan and his torchbearer, was still in this world, and all references to Ali Akbar Khansaheb in this work are made in that light.*

History is replete with great patriots, reformers, saint-musicians and other such beings who have left behind their pioneering impresses on posterity by the strength of their will and determination. And Padmavibhushan Ustad Allauddin Khan was one of them. Decades after his passing, he remains as bright a star as ever in the musical sky. Allauddin Khan embodied a history in himself. It is said that Arjuna (heroic figure in the epic *Mahabharata*) was also named Sabyasachi (meaning"ambidextrous") because he could fire his mighty arrows with both hands. Interestingly, Arjuna was an accomplished musician as well. Allauddin Khan was often called a "Sabyasachi of music" as he could also play musical instruments adeptly with either hand. Not only an outstanding genius in music, he was a unique personality in the entire realm of the arts.

He demonstrated the subtle relationship between life and the fine arts, between sound and soul, and between expression and language. The secret of his success was years of undaunted, unabated and rigorous sadhana (disciplined practice). His music was untainted by the smear of greed or fame.

Allauddin Khan was popularly known amongst his disciples and other music lovers as '**Baba**' (affectionate term meaning "father"). He was a veritable symbol of strength, encouragement and pure dedication. It is said that Ustad Allauddin Khan bathed in the "Svara Samudra" (the sea of melody). Honest and impartial in judgment, and a perfect master of his field, he was a real ascetic in simplicity and sincerity of devotion, and considered a prince amongst men, exemplifying a truly virtuous life.

To him, each note of a *Raga* (fully developed melodic structure beyond scales and modes – the basis for Indian Classical music) was a living entity. It seemed that when he played each of the notes, it crystallized into its own sublime form. For this wizard of the *sarod* (Allauddin Khan's primary instrument) there was a deep interrelationship between virtuosity and the realization of feelings inherent in the notes themselves.

At this point, the role of the teacher (guru) in Indian music needs addressing. It is said that without showing proper respect towards the guru, there is little possibility for one to learn music to an appreciable extent. The great Allauddin Khan never failed to acknowledge, with the greatest of humility, the master musicians from whom he learned, and by whose inspiration and teaching he was able to attain such lofty heights.

EARLY PERIOD

BIRTH

There are many controversies about the exact year of his birth. Some scholars such as Harendra Kishore Roy Chowdhury and several others consider 1881 as Baba's year of birth. However, some others place his year of birth as far back as 1862.

Ustad Allauddin Khan himself, in a letter from Maihar on May 18, 1956 to one of his favorite disciples, Shri Rebati Ranjan Debnath, gave out his age then as 90 years. Further, in 1958 when Baba was honored with the title of *Padmabhushan* by Babu Rajendra Prasad (the President of India at that time), his age was mentioned as 92. Thus it can be surmised that the year of Allauddin Khan's birth was most likely 1866.

Allauddin Khan belonged to a middle class family of *Badyakars* (professional instrumental musicians), who lived by providing music in various places on special occasions such as festivals, marriage ceremonies and the like. There were other classes of rural musicians, called *Dhoolis* (percussionists who played on *Dhol* (double-headed barrel-type folk drum)), *Bauls* (minstrel singers who were also players of instruments such as *sarinda, dotara, ektara, khanjari*, etc.) and others. At this same time, Khansaheb's family took to farming as well, as they had enough land and property with which to enterprise in profitable ventures.

Allauddin was affectionately called Alam in his childhood. In his somewhat more advanced years, people in general addressed him with the respectful term "Baba", as already referred to in the foregoing pages. His nephews lovingly called him *Lal Jetha* (beloved elder uncle – "lal": dear; "jetha": father's elder brother).

Allauddin's father Sadhu Khan was not liked by his father Madar Hussain Khan because Sadhu Khan did not show much interest in academic education, his primary inclination having been towards music. As far as music was concerned, Sadhu Khan was fortunate enough to have had a good teacher in the person of the distinguished musician Kashim Ali Khan of the Senia *gharana*. *(Gharana – lineage)* The *guru* gave his disciple good grounding in *sitar*. Sadhu Khan had also had the privilege of being associated with other celebrated musicians of the time in the state of Tripura, like Haidar Hussain Khan, Keshab Babu, the legendary Jadu Bhatt and other such masters.

Allauddin's father played sitar for his own pleasure and that of his family. Allauddin's elder brother Aftabuddin was a very talented and versatile musician who also did not perform professionally, but played solely to give vent to the melody and rhythm of music that he felt in his innermost being. In his later years, Aftabuddin became a Fakir, or spiritual mendicant, who was revered by Hindus and Muslims equally. The reputed musicians, Ram Kanai Seal and Ram Dhan Seal, who were the state musicians of Tripura at that time, trained Aftabuddin in the art.

Even at a tender age, because of his prodigious talent, Alam could pick up musical material by simply overhearing the recitals given by his father and the Seal brothers. In the later part of his life, he would pass on these musical quotes to his legacy. Alam's musical aptitudes were further kindled and deepened, as he continued listening to his father's sitar and his brother's facile handing of a variety of instruments, including the flute, harmonium, tabla, pakhawaj, and dotara. The boy often stole into the small music room to try his hands on some of his elder brother's musical instruments. Whenever caught red-handed in the act of playing music secretly, he was invariably punished for this transgression. However, matters grew more serious than this for the family. The idea that Alam, so keenly inclined to practicing musical exercises, might eventually take to this not-so-very-respectable art as a profession, filled his parents with great forebodings. At that time, the profession of music did not usually bring prestige or respect, unless one was a renowned master at the court of a king or such other exceptions. Thus, his parents were determined to put an end to such endeavors. However, despite their efforts, Alam's heart's ambition, which nothing could destroy or even dampen, would meet its fulfillment in the years to come.

Acts during childhood by great achievers are often indicators of the miraculous developments of the later years. An example of one such incident follows: one day Allauddin's mother Harasundari Khatoon divulged a secret to her husband concerning their boy Alam. It seems that the prodigy, while sucking from his mother's breast, used to take the breast onto his head, off and on, to use the bosom as a sort of tabla, as though he was providing time-keeping for his father's sitar playing. Sadhu Khan was both amazed and amused upon hearing this strange account and predicted a great future for Alam as a musician.

Alam began attending school at the age of five. It was the same institution as his brother Aftabuddin's, and the two brothers traveled to and from the school together.

At home, Alam had to dress up the *hookah* (hubble-bubble for smoking) of his elder brother who got the younger one to have a puff now and then so that the secret of his own smoking habit would not reach the ears of their superiors. Soon Alam became addicted to tobacco. He enjoyed his hookah till his final days. Aftabuddin had some other such activities and involvements which Alam had to look after as well. Aftabuddin took advantage of Alam's kindness regularly and often scolded his younger brother even in trifling matters. All such things began to make life seem bleak and charmless for Alam.

Alam resented his elder brother's undue interference into his affairs. Aftabuddin interfered with Alam's activities unnecessarily. Once, when Alam thought of leaving home and devoting his whole life to music, Aftabuddin, who enjoyed more influence with the family than himself, exposed Alam's intentions and the family, of course, refused to let him go. The parents expected Alam to concentrate on his studies at school regularly above anything else.

Allauddin shone in his academic life. However, although he was very studious, he could not deny his irrepressible attraction for music, and was eager to rid himself of the tutelage of his brother. He was ever on the lookout for a way to escape.

There was a famous temple of Lord Shiva in the village where Allauddin lived. The village itself – Shibpur – was named after this shrine. The temple flourished because sufficient property and finances had been endowed upon it.

Many devotees expressed their piety with musical presentations, both vocal and instrumental, in front of Lord Shiva. Alam found in its charged environment a source of great inspiration. He began visiting the Shiva temple daily, attending worship and taking *prasada* (sacramental food offerings to the deity).[1] The temple was visited by great sadhus (sages) and saints from all over India as a favored place of pilgrimage. Alam's burning love for music was further stoked by his regular attendance at the temple, which resounded with sublime sounds of musical expression much of the time. His religious bent of mind also accounted for his regular visits to the temple. He sometimes joined sadhus or musicians in their performances, giving them accompaniment on the tabla or singing with them. According to Ustad Allauddin Khan, Lord Shiva Himself appeared to him occasionally and blessed him with gifts of music.

The time of attending school and that of worshiping at the temple overlapped. Alam preferred to visit the temple rather than attend school, both because of his spiritual inclinations and his ardent love for music. He was hard put to keep his frequent visits from his parents. The latter would not have known about it had not the headmaster of the school lodged a complaint against him. He had been absent from school for six straight months. The headmaster informed his parents and himself came to Alam's house to know about his actual goings on. He not only condemned the boy's habit of keeping away from school, but also insisted that his parents not discontinue their son's education because he was a student of great promise.

Allauddin's parents were stupefied at this information about his truancy because they had thought that he had been regularly going to school. Alam actually used to set out from home daily on his way to school at the appointed hour and also came back home in the afternoon as any other boy would do after school hours. Upon hearing this unexpected news from the headmaster, Alam's parents became anxious to find out his real whereabouts during school time. His father followed him the next day without Alam's knowledge. Sadhu Khan's stealthy pursuit let him to the temple and he discovered his son engrossed in musical performances there. He was quite surprised to see his son's keen interest in the devotional activities.

Confused, Sadhu Khan returned home. When Alam returned, his father inquired about his activities. Alam admitted to his faults without hesitation. And, further exemplifying great moral courage, he announced his determination not to change his routine, which had become usual at that time.

His father, being a musician himself, did not take much offense at his son's ways, though he did not approve. However, his mother Harasundari Khatoon took it as an offense and punished him severely for his misconduct. Alam was barred from going outside the house altogether. He was not even given food for a couple

---

[1]   "Sangeet Prasanga" by Mobarek Hussain (son of Allauddin's youngest brother Ayat Ali).

of days. Nevertheless, he was so firm in his resolve that even these drastic steps could not deter him.

After being informed of all these incidents, Allauddin's eldest sister Madhumalati Khatoon, who lived close by and had a great affection for Alam, came to her parents' house. She took her brother to her own place with the idea that she would change his inclinations and habits through love and affection, but it was also in vain. Alam held his ground and did not pay any heed to her advice. After a few days, he had to come back home at the express desire of his ailing mother.

Obstacles and opposition made him more adamant than ever. After his return from the relatively comforting home of his sister, Alam looked to run away in search of higher musical attainments.

Allauddin was now eight years old. The more his parents and other guardians attempted to force him to mind his studies only, the more the boy shrank back from them. He was possessed solely to become a musician of the highest levels. Thus, the inevitable came one day, when he left the house without anyone's knowledge and ran away to a neighboring village.

In this town, he got himself admitted into a party of roving musicians which was led by a very well known player of the *dhol* (though the drums known as *dhol* or *dholak* are found all over India in different sizes and shapes, the type mentioned here is indigenous to Bengal). Alam told the musicians that he was left with nobody to look after him; they took pity upon the distraught boy and took him in their group. He then traveled with the group of performers wherever they went for their engagements. In this way, one day along with the party of musicians, the boy reached the city of Dhaka, the present day capital of Bangladesh. During his stint with the musical troupe, Alam had become trained in playing proficiently several types of drums, such as the *dhol, tabla* and *pakhawaj*. He also mastered the *shahnai* (double-reeded oboe-like instrument) and some other "blown" instruments, namely, clarinet, cornet and trumpet, all while working in the troupe. His sojourn in Dhaka was for quite a few months – first with the troupe and then, when the band had left, by himself. He never had any contact with his family during this time. Neither did he write to them nor did his relations come to know his whereabouts. From here, he proceeded to Barisal, where he met with Abdul Gaffoor Khan and Sital Chandra Mukharjee. Sital Chandra was as mad about music as Alam. He became one of the most prominent Esraj (fretted bowed instrument) players of Bengal in course of time. Allauddin spent nearly two years in this manner, moving from place to place, and trying his luck. He went to the Seal brothers, who were musicians at the court of His Highness, the Ruler of Tripura. One of Seals was a violinist. Alam was accepted as a student of the instrument, and stayed for a while in the house of his *guru* in the village of Bangora in Comilla learning violin. All such pursuits found their limits however, and in the end, he returned to his family home because of frustration, as his hopes could not be realized.

Allauddin now became eager to visit the Western parts of India, which were famous seats of music and other fine arts. Alam's exceedingly quick progress was a good enough cause for his moving elsewhere in search of still higher and finer training and great achievements. He had reached his emotional limit with the harassment he had to regularly meet with at home. It only helped to further strengthen his resolve to fight against all odds, however heavy.

Once again, he found another opportunity to run away. He took the door key from his mother, who was fast asleep, and appropriated a portion of money from the family treasury. He bowed down at his mother's feet to take her blessings before his departure.

Seeking to be at peace with his conscience now full of qualms and remorse at having been forced by circumstances to carry away part of the family wealth, Alam looked to unburden his feelings on the bank of the holy river Brahmaputra.

His future was shrouded in the darkness of uncertainty. He had deserted his home at this tender age of fourteen, exemplifying his indomitable will. Taking a steamer and then the train, he eventually reached Calcutta.

Allauddin was stymied upon seeing the busy and well-dressed people of the metropolis. He was lost in the crowd. Loitering here and there, he reached the bank of the Ganges. All of his belongings were stolen from him there, while he had fallen asleep. However, not being one to be so easily disheartened, Alam continued on undaunted, with the same enthusiasm for his mission as ever before.

During these early days in Calcutta, Allauddin was helped by a saint. The holy man directed the youth to a place where he could have his meals for a quite a long while without paying any money. A gentleman helped him in finding a night shelter. It was in the verandah of a doctor (popularly known as Kedar doctor).

He whiled away three months without any gain. Soon afterwards however, his prayers seemed to begin to bear fruit, as fortuitous opportunities began to appear in Alam's life.

Chapter 2

WITH GURUS (TEACHERS)

IT WAS BY chance that Alam encountered a young man who was seeking treatment and happened to visit the dispensary where he stayed.

The man was sympathetic to Alam and took pity upon him for his plight. Seeing the man curious to know about the cause of his trouble, Alam recounted his story with marked emphasis on that which was burning within. In the end, the young man offered his sincere cooperation as he was throrougly taken by Alam's impassioned appeal for help in the fulfillment of his ardent mission.

The next day, the youth obtained his mother's permission to invite Alam to his house. His mother received Alam warmly. In fact she doted upon him. However, Alam observed restraint and simply reminded her that before bestowing her affection upon him she should know about his parentage. He disclosed that he was a Mohamedan. She simply brushed aside his protestation, remarking, "Oh, there's nothing wrong in it. A child, whatever his religion may be, is a precious angel." She further remarked that she did not admit of any restrictions or scruples because of religion or caste. A person should not be excluded from love and affection merely because of artificial considerations of caste or religion. The mother of the young man gave Alam a mat to sit on and served him delicious food with maternal affection.

She was also amazed to notice Alam's burning desire for music even at that young age. She asked him to sing a song. He agreed and sang a devotional song he had formerly learned at the Shiva Temple in his native village. The noble woman found great pleasure in listening to his sweet and melodious voice, and the style with which he sang. She was yet another person in Alam's early life to have predicted a brilliant future for him as a thoroughly accomplished musician. She gave him her wholehearted blessings. As it turned out, the woman was herself a skilled musician, the reason for her taking such a keen interest in him. She took exception to a social more of the day and went out of her way to go to the other apartments of the house to contact her husband Bireshwar Babu – a thing which a *purddanasshin* lady, meaning – one respecting the "veil system," would have seldom done in those days. But her extreme eagerness to be of help to Alam had her adopt that unusual course. Immediately upon finding him, she implored her husband to do whatever he could to help the boy, who was mad with music. She also did not omit to guarantee absolutely good conduct on the part of Alam, who was then no better than a street urchin. She earnestly pressed Bireshwar Babu to take the trouble to introduce Alam to his own guru Gopal Chandra Bhattacharya, nicknamed Nulo Gopal for his unusually disproportionately sized hands. Bireshwar Babu, in his turn, had already caught the sound of Alam's sonorous voice when he had been singing inside just moments before, and found it naturally attractive and pleasing. His wife's praise for the musical talent of the boy and her pressing request to take Alam under his protective wings simply bore out his own impression and estimation.

Shortly thereafter, Bireshwar Babu took Alam to Nulo Gopal, who was then the retained musician of the palace of Maharaja Jotindra Mohan Tagore of Pathuriaghata near Jorashanko in Calcutta. Upon arriving at Nulo Gopal's house, Alam became spellbound at the sight of affluence and the grand manner of comforts under a single roof. The master musician was one of the most famous Bengali singers of his time, and was a very devout and orthodox Hindu.

Nulo Gopal noticed Allauddin's zeal, enthusiasm and talent for music. However, he forewarned the boy that as he himself had learned music through the very hard traditional method, so also would Alam have to undergo training at Nulo Gopal's hands in the same way. That is to say, the talented young man would have to learn and practice nothing other than the *sargams, paltas,* and *murchhana* (solfeggio, patterns, and scales and exercises) for a full twelve years. Only then would he start teaching Alam all the traditional compositions. This grooming was to begin after the initial stern phase of 12 years, which, although a very long time, no doubt, would give Alam the solid foundation he needed for his art.

Alam agreed to the arrangements and devoted himself to his training with single-mindedly. He was first taught the lesson of *swaragram* (fundamental sequences of notes) by his *guru* Nulo Gopal.

Allauddin enjoyed this work. He used to take the *tanpura* (stringed drone instrument) in one hand and play Bayan (the bass drum of the *tabla* pair) with the other. Simultaneously, he tapped *matras* (beats) with one foot and *tala* (full rhythmic cycles) with the other one. After practicing like this he became extraordinarily accurate in tala (attained mastery over rhythmic cycles of any configuration). He was praised by those who would hear him, often profusely, and his *guru* (teacher) was proud of the stellar disciple. Alam would get up at 2 a.m. daily and practice with his *guru* until 5 a.m.

Nulo Gopal was ungrudging in imparting knowledge to his disciples unlike the Ustads (master musicians) of those days. Alam was impressed by his guru's character and felt blessed.

During the time of his training under Nulo Gopal, Alam had to assume a Hindu name – Manmohan Dey – in accordance with his *guru's* wish.

Alam learned the variations of *swaragram* known as *palta* (transposable patterns) from one Ganga Ram Thakur. Ganga Ram was one of Nulo Gopal's senior and favorite disciples. It was he who also cooked food for the master. By his virtuous character and austerity, Alam endeared himself to both of them. Alam outshone all other trainees at the place through his intense practice. He had wholly imbibed everything offered to him from the rich storehouse of knowledge held by Nulo Gopal and Ganga Ram. Alam derived additional impetus to excel because of the loving care given towards him by these two great artists.

Allauddin was captivated by the natural grace of Nulo Gopal's personality and character. He was a great artist who, although provided with all the good things of life, appeared quite indifferent to worldly pleasures. Nulo Gopal was, indeed, the first man who impressed Alam with both his musical knowledge and immaculate character. He played a considerable part in preparing Allauddin's future career as a great maestro. Alam's training received its consummation and finishing from Ustad Wazir Khan of the then Rampur Sate in Uttar Pradesh some years later.

Nulo Gopal was an ideal kind of *guru*. He taught and looked after Alam with fatherly care and affection. Once he asked about Alam's arrangement for his meals. Alam told his guru everything about the matter. Nulo Gopal became filled with pity and sympathy. Being a retained musician, he exerted his influence to have Alam's boards arranged in the palace of the Tagores. From then on, Alam had his meals there continuously for 7 years.

MARRIAGE

Now Allauddin began believing that he could actually achieve his goal. However, other events would transpire first. As he was becoming settled in Calcutta, suddenly his brother Aftabuddin arrived in Calcutta, along with his father-in-law Mian Gulam Mohammed, to take Alam back to their native village. Before reaching Calcutta, Aftabuddin had searched all conceivable places noted for classical music to find his younger brother.

Nulo Gopal was reluctant to allow Alam to leave him at that time, and he said that this kind of break in training could be a detriment to Alam's future progress and career. However, the relatives pleaded with Nulo Gopal repeatedly, saying that they would send Alam back to him after the visit to his mother. Even though Alam longed to see his mother and elder sister, he was unwilling to go back, knowing that it would likely have negative consequences. Yet, in the end, he could not continue to refuse and had to succumb to his elder brother's pressure. After seven long years, he returned home. All of the members of his family were happy to see him again, particularly his mother and affectionate sister.

The elders of the family as a whole were now pressing Alam to marry, partly out of the hope that marriage would prevent Alam from leaving home again.

In those times, parents decided upon and settled the marital ties of their sons and daughters long before the actual dates of marriages – in some instances even during their childhood, and, in some cases, even before they were actually born. Allauddin's father had made such an arrangement with a family friend, Bashir Khan (at the time that Bashir Khan's wife had given birth to a girl), that Sadhu Khan would have Bashir Khan's daughter as the bride of Allauddin after both of them had grown up.

Aftabuddin had Alam's date of marriage fixed without the knowledge of the future groom. Then one day, just before the time the wedding was to take place, Aftabuddin took his younger brother to Raipur, justifying it with a pretext that it was on the way to Calcutta, where he was being expected back by his music teacher. Aftafuddin disclosed his real motive afterwards. Alam was vehement upon hearing the truth and refused to marry in this way. His brother reminded him that it would not be appropriate to go back on the word of their father, who had already settled his marriage with Bashir Khan's daughter. Further, he assured his brother that after the marriage, Alam could easily get back to Calcutta for further training. Although he was resentful of the ruse, the prospect of going back to his teacher gave Allauddin a sort of consolation. And after all, Aftabuddin himself was not wholly responsible for it, because originally it was the desire of his parents. Allauddin married eight-year-old Madan Manjari, one of the beauties of that locality. He himself was hardly 15 years of age then. The marriage was completed in a manner befitting to the respective families and the society of the time.

The next day some post-marriage ceremonies had to be observed. However, in the dead of night, when Alam found his bride in deep sleep, the idea flashed upon his mind that he might become captivated by his wife's beauty and love, which might stand between him and his great mission of becoming a first-class master musician. No sooner had this idea occurred to him that he thoroughly made up his mind to flee back to Calcutta to complete his training. He then collected all his wife's ornaments with heartbreaking remorse. But it seemed that there was no other way except through this questionable act to get money. And he needed a substantial amount as he had to buy a railway ticket for Calcutta and carry some amount for out-of-pocket expenses in the metropolis. It is obvious that this dubious course to get money, resorted to by an otherwise virtuous boy as he was known to have been, was simply because of his overwhelming passion for music, and could be said to be unavoidable in the course of the fulfillment of his destiny.

Allauddin left the area and traveled directly to Calcutta. He tried his very best to wipe out from his memory whatever ordeals he had had to pass through in the intervening period. It was like a bad dream. Determined to forge ahead, he proceeded to up any frivolous activities of life to attain his goal of achieving distinction in the world of music.

AGAIN IN SEARCH OF A GURU

Alam was eager to meet his *guru* Nulo Gopal as quickly as possible. He went to the master's house directly from the Sealdah railway station. However, he was surprised to find the house locked up. He went to the Tagore palace to contact Kiran Babu, an acquaintance of his guru, in order to ascertain Nulo Gopal's present whereabouts. He was stunned, as if hit by a bolt from the blue, at the sad and shocking news about his *guru's* passing. Nulo Gopal had died of cholera during this time. Kiran Babu further told him that because of Nulo Gopal having left no heir nor any will, all his things, including his house, now belonged to the Government.

Nulo Gopal's death was an irreparable loss for Alam. Hardly had his dream of becoming a great exponent of music started materializing when suddenly his mentor left him and the world forever. Nulo Gopal had cherished him with fatherly affection. Alam was at a loss to decide about his future. However, Allauddin possessed the fortitude and stamina to brace all manners of hardship and obstacles even at that age, particularly regarding his great trek to his lifelong vision to master the science and art of music. His painstaking ardor for music and, for that matter, for any cherished goal, was exemplary, worthy of emulation by all students at all times. His was a kind of *sadhana* (disciplined practice for a worthy endeavor) which admitted of no obstacle, however formidable.

Some days afterwards, Alam again went to Kiran Babu to seek advice regarding how he should proceed next. This gentleman was yet another of his sincere well-wishers. He was eager to know what a young trainee like Alam would do in the changed circumstances. Alam had by then considerably developed his ear and sensitivity for music, thanks to the excellent training at the expert hands of Nulo Gopal. He did not want to put a stop to his musical ambition midway and unrealized. However, looming large before him was the problem of finding a guru – a coach of the same caliber and accomplishment as the late Nulo Gopal. Alam could not find anyone up to his expectations and he decided at last to discontinue his course in vocal music and instead chose to change over to instrumental music. He disclosed his mind to Kiran Babu. Kiran Babu recommended him to approach Amritalal Dutta, known popularly as Habu Dutta, who belonged to the same family as Swami Vivekananda (a renowned Bengali saint/philosopher), for training in instrumental music. Habu Dutta was most likely a cousin brother of the great Swami. This master was proficient both in Indian and Western instrumental music. Sent to him with a word of high recommendation by Kiran Babu, the bereaved young man narrated his woeful story to Habu Dutta. The master was moved deeply.

Habu Dutta consoled Alam and gave him a firm assurance of all possible help for the fulfillment of his ambition. He took the youth as his disciple and eventually came to prize his *guru-shishya* (teacher-disciple) relationship with Alam throughout his life.

Habu Dutta began giving him advanced training in violin, which Alam had learned at the beginning of his training years from the Seal brothers, back in the village of Bangora. He purchased a costly violin at that time which caused a heavy drain on his purse. Nevertheless, there was no other course. Alam was already trained in the rudiments of music, such as *swaragram, palta*, etc. Now, he was ready to learn the 360 versions of altering variations (*palta*). With the background of substantial training in vocal music as well, he continued to receive more musical knowledge, this time through the violin, from Habu Dutta. Within a few months, he was able to play the aforementioned *paltas* on violin very swiftly. Within a year, he had gained considerable mastery over the instrument. Suffice it to say, Habu Dutta was very pleased. The evidence of this inordinate ability to quickly gain command of this very difficult musical instrument encouraged Alam to pursue and master other instruments, and in quick succession.

It was a matter of chance that young Alladuddin came across Mr. Lobo Probhu. A highly knowledgeable and master musician, Lobo Probhu was engaged by the Government of India as a state musician in Calcutta, the city which was the capital of India at that time. Alam was at the moment residing in a house in the Bahubazar area close to Lobo Probhu's quarters. Lobo Probhu's wife was also a highly accomplished musician and considered to be a very good pianist. Alam often overheard beautiful solo or duet recitals played by the virtuoso couple. Alam was amazed to hear the Western approach of music, which had an arresting lure to him as well. He at once decided to study Western music, as a competent teacher was there in the person of Lobo Probhu. He visited Mr. Lobo's place several times but could not contact him. He dared not open his mind to Mrs. Lobo when he met her. He bade her good-bye for that day and came back disappointed. However, his repeated visits to the virtuoso's house to speak to him, although without success, made him familiar with the Mem Sahib (her ladyship – a term usually associated with white women).

One day, Alam was preparing to go to his teacher Habu Dutta's house for lessons and he caught the glimpse of the Lobo couple basking in the sun. Alam took advantage of their being available and walked straight inside their house with the violin in hand. But Mr. Lobo did not care to notice him. Mrs. Lobo was curious to know the name of his teacher. Alam told her about Habu Dutta. Hearing the name of the eminent musician, she asked him to play. Alam performed well. The couple was pleased and praised his efforts.

But Alam was not satisfied with so little. As he was already familiar with Mrs. Lobo, he ventured to ask her to present his case to her husband. She eventually answered back that Mr. Lobo would be pleased to teach him, but had no time to spare. However, Alam paid no heed to her excuse. He entreated the Sahib (Mr. Lobo – "sahib" usually meaning "sir", similar to the Italian "signor") again and again. Mr. Lobo became irritated and clearly told Alam to understand that he was not a man to teach a "nigger" (a black native), and then ordered him to leave. Alam came back disheartened. However, Mrs. Lobo had taken kindly to the youth and wanted to make up for the unpleasantness created by her husband.

Mrs. Lobo asked him to come to her place daily at 1 p.m. for lessons in Western music. At that time her husband would be out for his work. She taught him many things with great care. In due course she again pleaded to her husband to reconsider Alam's case. At last, Mr. Lobo changed his mind and found some spare time for Alam. By the joint effort of the Lobos he advanced in Western music as well. They were extremely pleased with his character, work ethic and zeal for learning new things. In the end, the Lobos taught him without any reservation, and Alam learned exceptionally quickly. The couple was amazed at his power to grasp musical material and gave him their blessings and wished that he might achieve success in life. Allauddin continued to learn the Indian approach to violin from yet another teacher, Amar Das. After that training he went to a renowned Bengali Hindu clarinet player who lived in a locality predominantly inhabited by Muslims.

Alam then took to the *shehnai* (double-reed oboe-like instrument), which was taught to him by the famous Ustad Hazari Khan. He went on to study *mridanga*, also known as *pakhawaj* (double-headed barrel drum for the *Dhrupad* style of classical music), which is one of the most complex and difficult percussion instruments to master. He received his training in *tabla* (the most popular of the North Indian classical drums) and *mridanga* continuously for six years from the eminent Nandalal Babu. He quickly became adept at these percussion instruments, partly because of his having been taught *dhol* (double-headed barrel drum for folk music) by the famous *dhol* player Abdul Gafoor in his childhood.

Before shifting to any new instrument, Alam invariably completed the course of training being given to him for the instrument he was presently studying to the utmost satisfaction of the teacher of that instrument. He did not shift his interest for the sake of a change only, but for the fulfillment of his burning desire to learn music in every branch.

Habu Dutta was the driving force behind his eager interest in learning varieties of instruments. This *guru* of Allauddin never tired of recommending his pupil to anyone at any time, whenever necessary. He stood by his disciple in his trials and his grim struggle for existence, as he loved Alam like his son. Alam's noble conduct and sincere regard for his teachers held him in a high place in all of their hearts.

During these times, Allauddin experienced financial hardships constantly. Finally, he disclosed his plight to Habu Dutta. Upon hearing this, his guru took him to the Minerva Theater, a popular dramatic venue and institution of that time. It was managed by the celebrated actor-playwright, Girish Ghosh. Habu Dutta introduced Alam as one of his favorite disciples. Because of Habu Dutta's highly respected recommendation, Alam was hired by the Minerva Theater with little objection.

He was appointed to help the music director of the theater with composition and directing, as well as taking care of the various instruments of the theater. Within a few days, Alam's boss recognized his talent and was very satisfied with his work, skill and potential. Alam had won the heart of all of the senior artists and musicians of the Minerva with his sincerity of purpose.

It was here that Allaudin learned the technique of setting music for the stage or drama. Girish Ghosh – the head of the institution – became aware of his musical abilities and was thoroughly taken by his genius-like accomplishments. Girish Ghosh soon invited Alam into his close circle and endowed him with a name of endearment, Prasanna Kumar Biswas.

It was during this period that a spiritual encounter of the rarest kind happened to Allauddin, as he came in contact with Shri Ramkrishna Paramahansa, the great saint of Bengal and India in the late 19th century. Girish Ghosh, the head of the theater, was one of the most historically written about disciples of the enlightened Shri Ramakrishna, whose teachings on the unity of spiritual paths would eventually influence the course of spirituality in the public eye, not only in India but the rest of the world, particularly through his most well-known disciple, Swami Vivekananda, widely recognized as the first Indian to bring the wisdom of India to the West.

Allauddin was by now well placed in the theater and his monetary problem was partially solved. But owing to his moral scruples and religious bent of mind he was not able to fit himself into the atmosphere prevailing in the world of the theater in those days. Persons connected with the professional stage, more often than not, were of questionable moral habits, usually linked with alcohol addiction and sexual promiscuity. Alam kept himself detached from such temptations with great tenacity. His strength of character intact, he managed to disassociate himself from the morally corrupt.

In time, Allauddin began considering shunning the rather destructive company of actors and others of the theater. He unburdened his innermost feelings to his mentor Girish Ghosh. Girish Babu ("babu" – gentleman, or "sir") was impressed by his keen sense of morality and at once agreed to let him sever connections with his institution, although Alam had become almost indispensable for him. Girsh Babu advised him to resign and suggested that he dedicate his life to the uplifting of classical music. He gave Allauddin his blessings and wished him a happy and prosperous life.

At this point, Alam began to believe that he had already become a musician of consummate skill because of his expansive knowledge in almost all of the instruments in popular use at that time in India. This pride came about partly due to the showering of praise and appreciation upon him by his colleagues and the public at large. As well, he considered going back to his family and make amends with his deserted wife, but he changed this idea afterwards.

Allauddin was informed of a musical conference which was to be held during the Dusserah festival under the auspices of the family of the wealthy land-baron of Muktagachha, who bore the title of Maharaja (king). Many top-ranking musicians were to participate in conference. Proud and feeling that he was equal to the task, Alam decided to take part in that musical soiree, as he believed that with his knowledge of different instruments, he could make a significant impression in the conference.

Alam managed to reach the *durbar* (court) of Raja Jagat Kishore Acharya of Muktagachha and expressed his desire for participation in the conference by virtue of his experience of fifteen years in the field of music. With some misgivings, the Raja gave his consent. He ordered an orderly of the court to take care of Allauddin's boarding and lodging. The young maestro was asked to present himself at the court next morning at exactly 8 a.m. Some of the courtiers did not hesitate to remark that this young man must have gone mad to vie with the outstanding musicians of India. True to his nature, Allauddin did not take notice of the sarcastic remarks.

The next day, when he arrived at the *durbar* with all his instruments, the court was already filled to capacity with ardent lovers of Indian classical music. The Raja had his seat at a prominent place, flanked by his courtiers, seated according to their ranks. Alam was quite sure of his success in the gathering. In an atmosphere charged with an air of expectation of the highest levels of musical expression, many wondered how this unlikely candidate, as Allauddin surely was, would fare. To a hushed crowd, it was announced that the musical function was going to be inaugurated by the *sarod* maestro Ustad Ahmed Ali.

This was the first time that Allauddin had heard the sarod (plucked stringed lute with a fretless fingerboard). It was also the first time that the very tuning of an instrument enraptured him. As Ustad Ahmed Ali turned the tuning pegs and struck the strings of the sarod, Allauddin was caught in a trance by the instrument's beautiful sound, and began to see his own limited capabilities.

At 8 a.m., the great and knowledgeable master Ustad Ahmed Ali began playing. The audience was spellbound by a magnificent interpretation of Raga Darbari Todi. The stellar performance lasted for 5 hours, without stop. Ustad Ahmed Ali's magnificent display not only revealed Allauddin's marked inferiority in the face of music of such high quality, but it also moved him profoundly with its depth. Tears rolling down both his cheeks, Allauddin lost himself in Ustad Ahmed Ali's performance. His self-conceit and vanity vanished. He came back to his senses after the Ustad had stopped. He approached the Ustad and touched his feet in great reverence, and fervently appealed to Ahmed Ali Khan to accept him as his disciple. He asked for the Raja's favor in this regard as well. The Raja was a generous, yet sober minded man. He was taken by Alam's repeated plea. Seeing the Raja's inclination to help Allaudin and himself moved by the youths petition, the *sarod* maestro agreed to accept the young musician as his disciple. The formalities of *nara* or *ganda* ceremony (symbolic thread tying linking teacher to disciple) were completed at the expense of Raja Jagat Kishore Acharya's estate. The king presented Allauddin with a sarod to encourage this young and promising artist, and also as a token of his affection. Thus ended Allauddin's long search for a guru of Indian Classical Music who could give him proper guidance on a classical instrument.

Ustad Ahmed Ali's father Ustad Abid Ali was also a sarod player and one of great distinction and celebrity at the *durbar* of the Nawab of Rampur in the province of Uttar Pradesh (in North India). His forefathers were court musicians of Bahadur Shah, the last Mughal emperor.

Ahmed Ali was in the service of the nobleman Seth Duli Chand Marwari of Ghughudanga (near Calcutta.) The Seth was obsessed with music. He retained the services of other musicians of great repute as well, such as Tara Bai, Maujuddin Khan, Badal Khan and Ganpat Rao.

Allauddin was asked by Ahmed Ali to reside with him at his home for the convenience of training. But whenever Ahmed Ali went out for performances, Allauddin was made to look after the household duties. He had to cook, sweep the place, wash clothes and do a great many other chores. He was taught to prepare special Indian dishes by his new *guru*. Owing to his inexperience in cooking, he sometimes spoiled the meals of his Ustad (maestro). As Alam did not eat meat, he could not taste the food before serving. He was severely scolded by Ahmed Ali for his culinary blunders. Alam was treated more as a butler than a disciple of music by his Ustad. He bore all such humiliation to win the favor of his great teacher which, however, he never got.

Besides doing household chores, Alam often accompanied Ahmed Ali's *sarod* recital as his tabla accompanist. And, whenever there was a program, Alam also played on violin. By that time, he had earned the reputation of being an accomplished violinist. Alam typically earned 25 to 30 rupees for his accompaniment. Thus he now had a regular source of income through the cooperation of his *guru*. Ahmed Ali deposited in Alam's care whatever of his own fees he received from performances. Alam kept an account of income and expense for his teacher. Ahmed Ali drew upon these funds whenever it was necessary.

Alam regularly listened in on his teacher's morning practices. Ahmed Ali would go to central Calcutta from time to time. During his absence Alam practiced all of the pieces of his guru's *riyaz* (practice session) from memory. He practiced secretly because it would be thought that he was stealing musical material from his Ustad. He learned and practiced such material during the four years he was with Ahmed Ali.

One day, Allauddin was secretly practicing *Darbari Todi*, the Ustad's favorite raga, when suddenly his teacher arrived, hearing him play from outside the closed door. Ahmed Ali was both surprised and furious and ordered Alam to open the door which he had bolted from inside. Alam opened it and the Ustad rebuked him, saying that he was a thief and a plunderer, who was stealing his valuable musical things. Alam apologized to him and promised not to behave in this manner any more. Ahmed Ali reminded him that the stage for Alam to learn or perform the *raga* in question had not yet been reached and that he needed to set his hands first.

In those days reputed musicians hesitated to impart their knowledge to their meritorious students outside the family. They kept the full repository limited to blood lineage only. Most musicians at that time were illiterate, puffed up with self-conceit, and were conservative in their thinking. If there were not any suitable descendants, the beautiful characteristics of their musical lineage ended with their own deaths. Many schools of music with precious wisdom ended in this way.

Ahmed Ali was not an exception to this conservative way of thinking. Owing to such, he did not teach Allauddin a single bit of the treasured material willfully. Despite all his efforts Allauddin could not draw much attention from Ahmed Ali. The master was unwilling to teach advanced things to Alam as he feared the boy would outdo him. He kept the young musician in the dark by one pretense or another. He never taught Alam *alap* (rendition of raga without accompaniment of a rhythmic instrument), the most profound, beautiful and the most respected part of the performance of a *raga*, where the artist's mastery of understanding a particular raga and its full expression is realized. Ahmed Ali kept Alam's training limited to *vilambit* and *drut gats* (slow and fast compositions, which come after the presentation of the *alap*). During those hard years, purely due to his exceptional talent, Alam learned almost solely by overhearing his Ustad. He refined his knowledge through relentless practice.

Allauddin accompanied his Ustad as his caretaker wherever he went. He went to central Calcutta and Agra several times, places where Ahmed Ali met with his lady lovers Guaharjan and Malkabai, respectively. These two women were also skilled vocalists. Alam had had the good fortune to hear their superb music, presented in different styles. It further enriched his musical knowledge.

The Ustad was fretful at Alam's progress. Out of his fear that Allauddin should surpass him, he wanted to be rid of him. And he thought that he had better do so at Rampur.

On the way to Rampur they visited Patna and Varanasi. At Patna they remained for one month as guests of the Nawab of Patna. Both teacher and disciple performed for the Nawab. They were rewarded with an Rs.2000 and Rs.1000 respectively. From there they went to Varanasi, considered the holiest city for Hindus, a place of hundreds of thousands of temples and shrines. There they performed many *sarod* and violin recitals, and sometimes Alam accompanied the Ustad on tabla as well. They collected a handsome amount of money. The entire amount was kept with Allauddin.

After that they came to their desired destination – Rampur. Ahmed Ali introduced Allauddin as his disciple to his parents. He touched their feet to show his respect. After the formalities of talks and other such things they had their meals. Alam thought it to be the proper time to return the money to his Ustad. He handed back to him Rs.10,000. Ahmed Ali and his parents were surprised at his loyalty and profusely spoke blessings upon him. As it turned out, the family in the beginning did not behave properly with Alam. Initially he had been kept in a hut adjacent to the lavatory. He felt sick of the stench, but he did not open his mouth about it. After returning the money, however, he was shifted to a better place. Although Ahmed Ali was happy that the money was kept securely, he was still reluctant to teach Alam.

Ahmed Ali planned to construct a brick house with that income. Alam continued to look after the household and did some manual labor as well. Such hardships ended up having him suffer from gastric troubles (an illness he suffered throughout his life). Eventually, Ahmed Ali's parents shifted to the new house, leaving Alam in the old one. But they continued to provide him with his meals.

It seems that Ahmed Ali was bent on getting rid of Alam. One day Ahmed's mother told Alam allegorically that if an illness could not be cured by a particular doctor, then the patient had to go to some other. It so happened now that Alam had picked up whatever Ahmed Ali had himself mastered during his whole life. Now for further advancement, he needed once again to look for another teacher. As he was witnessing an inclination in others to give him a cold shoulder, the task of finding a new guru was challenging indeed. Alam decided to ask Abid Ali (Ahmed Ali's father) himself about the prospects of finding a teacher. Abid Ali suggested the name of Ustad Wazir Khan, son of Ustad Amir Khan, the most famous *beenkar* of Northern India, for this purpose.

From then on Ahmed Ali's parents stopped providing boards for Alam, and the young man now had to move out. Ahmed Ali had returned to Calcutta by that time. Alam was stranded once again. He was left now with only 6 or 7 rupees out of the amount he had saved from the money he had earned before in the theater in Calcutta.

At this critical time, Alam had no one who would come to his aid. But he continued his to forge ahead out of his relentless enthusiasm and ardor for music. He knocked at the doors of almost all of the well-known musicians in Calcutta, meeting refusal after refusal, as he could not afford to satisfy their high expectations regarding fees and favors.

Regardless of the ardous circumstances, Alam clinged fast to his life-long ambition for musical brilliance. Even though he had misgivings, he eventually found the courage to try his luck with Ustad Wazir Khan, whom he had been lately fixing upon in his mind as his prospective *guru*. Every day he went to the gate of the palace where the master was enjoined, but each time was sent back unceremoniously by the porter. Alam, however, repeated this venture of coming and going in vain for no less than six months. It had been next to impossible to meet Wazir Khan.

Allauddin eventually broke down under the sheer weight of such cruel treatment, seemingly kept in store for him by destiny itself. He became exhausted both physically and mentally. He was given to thinking during these hard hours of his life that only death could bring the peace he sought. He had always been pricked by the thought of what people at home and around would think of him if he failed to achieve greatness. Alam bought two tolas (about 1 oz.) of opium and decided to end his life at a mosque where he would usually go to say his prayer.

So the despondent young man dragged himself to the mosque to carry out his plan, but right at that critical moment, a *Maulavi* (muslim sage) came upon him and eventually consoled his restless spirit, and then treated him to a meal afterwards. The *Maulavi* dissuaded him from his contemplated course of action and advised him to go on trying his luck till he attained success. For his part, the holy man promised that he would stand by Alam's side at times of difficulty. He encouraged him thusly in various ways, citing several pithy savings in the process such as, "None but the brave deserve the fair" and other such age-old morale boosting statements. Coming from the Maulavi, somehow these statements did not feel like cliches to the young man, and instead of discarding them as fanciful sayings, Alam decided to take the such advice to heart and carry on.

Alam now felt inclined to take the kind-hearted Maulavi into his confidence. He told him how he had hitherto failed to contact Ustad Wazir Khan even after trying time and again, and also how other teachers had as well refused to favor him.

The Maulavi felt great sympathy for Allauddin and drafted a letter on his behalf, addressed to the Nawab. The letter narrated Allauddin's ending up at wanting to commit suicide out of the tremendous desire to learn music from Ustad Wazir Khan, which became impossible to fulfill as he was stopped innumerably at the very gate of his palace by his doorkeepers. Driven to despair, he had plotted to take his own life. It was also mentioned in the letter that it was only the Nawab that could save this youth's life by intervening in the matter. The draft prepared by the Maulavi ended with praying for the Nawab's mercy.

He then advised Allauddin to pass it on into the hands of the Nawab himself by blocking his car, when the dignitary would come out from his palace in the evening for a pleasure ride.

Alam wanted to act upon the Maulavi's advice, but a proper opportunity was lacking. It would soon come.

One evening the Nawab Sahib was on his way to the theater. The piece for performance there was a creation of the Nawab's own teacher, the same maestro Ustad Wazir Khan, who had also achieved great distinction as a poet. The Nawab and his guards were driving in a horse-drawn limousine when it was suddenly blocked by Allauddin. He raised up his hands with a cry of agony. The driver and the guards came down to see who had dared to stop the Nawab's car. The guards tried to remove Alam out of the way unnoticed by their master, but they could not as the Nawab himself inquired about the matter to his head guard. He replied that a dirty and obstinate Bengali youth had been repeatedly asking for a meeting with His Highness, the Nawab of Rampur.

The Nawab ordered his men to bring Alam at once in front of him and the fated young man was produced before him. Alam showed due respect to His Highness and handed him over the petition authored by the Maulavi.

After going through the letter with the help of his A.D.C. in chief, the Nawab wanted to see the opium Alam had bought to kill himself. Alam showed it to him. The Nawab took the drug away from him and remarked that he was indeed a brave youth. He was impressed by his sincere desire for learning from Ustad Wazir Khan, failing which he was ready to destroy his own life. The Nawab canceled his program of going to the theater and went back to his residential palace known as "Hamid Manzil," taking Allauddin with him. He ordered his Home Secretary to request Wazir Khan to meet him when he would return after the drama performance was over.

Nawab Hamid Ali inquired about Alam's musical background, and the young musician detailed his musical history with his revered *gurus*, from Nulo Gopal to Ahmed Ali, the teachers from whom he had learned vocal as well as instrumental music. He also spoke of the various instruments which he had studied. He also described under what circumstances he had turned to instrumental music from vocal.

Inquiries over, Allauddin was asked to give a demonstration of his skill with instruments. A car was sent to Allauddin's residence to fetch his instruments. He first gave a vocal recital which was appreciated by the Nawab. His Highness told him that given his earnestness and devotion, there would be no difficulty for him to learn from Wazir Khan. Alam felt encouraged by this remark. He proceeded to play *sarod*. He performed a brief alap which he had learned by overhearing Ahmed Ali. The Nawab was extremely pleased to hear his violin. He remarked that he had not heard a violin recital of such a high standard as Allauddin's. Nawab Sahib was himself a famous musician, who had had a repository of 1000 *dhrupads* (poems based on Ragas in the oldest form of North Indian Classical Music – also known as "Dhrupad"). Compliments from such a person were indeed of the highest regard.

The Nawab asked him what more Allauddin wanted to learn from Ustad Wazir Khan. He simply replied, "beena" (the most respected of the plucked stringed instruments, believed to be thousands of years old – also known as Rudra Vina). The Nawab Hamid Ali Khan said that the Ustad did not teach that instrument to anyone else but a pupil related to him by blood, as Wazir Khan was held to an injunction in the matter of imparting lessons on beena. The stipulation was that the disciple must be either a son or some other person related to the teacher by blood. Wazir Khan believed that in case he acted otherwise, he might not be survived by a son or any other male heir.

After that the Nawab asked Alam whether he could accompany the Nawab's vocal recital on the violin. Alam gladly accepted that proposal. Pleased by his abilities, the Nawab asked Allauddin to accept service in his court, which he refused, saying that he was keener to learn more music than get employment. The Nawab sang a hori (a composition based on the life of Lord Krishna) in *raga Behag* – "*Yamuna jale, sakhi kaise jaun.*" Alam was enchanted to hear his melodious voice. The Nawab was an artist of a very high order indeed. He asked Alam to accompany him again in *tappa* (a semi-classical form with almost non-stop, fast and circuitous lines) to which, however, Allauddin could not do justice on violin.

Ustad Wazir Khan arrived there with the Home Secretary after some time. He asked the Nawab about the grounds for his taking such interest in an unknown boy. The Nawab sat beside this guru (a great honor for the musician) and gently enlightened him on the Bengali youth Alam and his apparent resolution to give up his own life if he could not find an opportunity to learn music from Wazir Khan. Hamid Ali Khan also spoke to his Ustad about Allauddin's rather commendable musical background. The young aspirant, in his turn, lay himself prostrate at Wazir Khan's feet as a gesture of great reverence. The Ustad could not but take interest in this adamant yet humble boy and eventually consented to teach him.

The *ganda* or *nara* ceremony (sacred thread-tying ceremony between teacher and disciple) was completed under the supervision of no less a person than the Nawab Hamid Ali Khan himself. Wazir Khan was also happy to know that Alam's father was a disciple of Wazir Khan's maternal uncle Ustad Kashim Ali Khan.

In the *nara* ceremony, costly jewelry, shawls and sweets were presented to Wazir Khan at the state's expense. According to tradition, the Ustad tied the *nara* (thread) first on the hand of Hamid Ali as he was his foremost disciple. He then tied the thread on Allauddin's hand. Certain vows had to be taken such as, (*i*) the student would never teach music to any undesirable elements, (*ii*) he would never keep evil company, (*iii*) he would never misuse music for any evil purpose and (*iv*) he would never teach any "dancing girl" (often the term for prostitutes, some of whom, at that time, were often accomplished classical musicians).

The news had spread all around that a Bengali youth had obstructed the way of the Nawab. The police came and inquired whether Alam had carried a bomb with him. The Nawab, at the time of the incident, had also inquired about the same thing, to which Allauddin had replied enigmatically that he had no reason to use for a bomb, if he was taught music properly. "But then, those bombs," Allauddin clarified, to a great sense of relief on the part of his interlocutors, "would not be bombs of destructive explosives, but of *svaras* (musical notes)."[2]

Thus Allauddin's long-cherished dream was fulfilled. He was told and promised that he would be taught *sarod, surrsringar* and *rabab*, but not *beena*. Alam gladly agreed. He was provided with a house which was near the residence of Ustad Wazir Khan. Allauddin's financial problem remained the same. He did not have money even for food. He ate as inexpensively and as healthily as possible.

---

[2]   "Amar Katha" by Ustad Allauddin Khan.

OTHER MAESTROS AT RAMPUR

With his living quarters almost adjacent to his teacher, Allauddin went to the residence of Wazir Khan daily in the morning and evening with his *sarod* and stood there for hours at a stretch. He used to reach the *guru's* house at 8 a.m. In keeping with the Nawab's advice, he served his Ustad in many ways. Allauddin supplied water in the mug in the guru's lavatory. After the Ustad's use of the toilet, he cleaned that place with some deodorants, etc. He cleaned and polished the Ustad's medals regularly. He did all such things for two years continuously. Very few could have gone through such hard experiences. But Alam held his patience. Even so, he did not achieve success making his Ustad feel inclined to give him music lessons. Having no other alternatives, Alam approached some other musicians of repute and tried to make progress in his career in his own way. Allauddin was well regarded by all such teachers because of his good standing with the Nawab, and because his manners were so amenable.

Allauddin went to bandmaster Raja Hussain of the Rampur state, who was the son of the famous *dhrupad* singer Khalipha Daulat Khan of Lucknow. Daulat Khan praised Alam upon hearing his music. At one time, after composing some pieces he gave them to Allauddin to check. Raja Hussain had had knowledge of *dhrupad* and *dhamar*, but he was not sufficiently skilled to prepare compositions on them for orchestra. He taught Alam many *dhrupads* and *dhamars*, and Allauddin expertly arranged the pieces for Raja Hussain's band, as he had been trained in this line by Habu Dutta. He eventually received an appointment as a regular violin player in that orchestra.

There was another musician who was a disciple and son-in-law of Kutub-ud-daula, a famous vocalist of the time. This man took to Allauddin and treated him with great affection. He taught the young man *dhrupad, dhamar, dadra* and other various types of vocal music of considerable complexity and intricacy. In return, Alam helped this teacher with the mundane things of daily life and work.

The band party of Rampur counted about 700 instrumentalists under its aegis. Mohammed Hussain Khan, the brother of Mustaq Hussain Khan's guru, was also one of the players in the orchestra. Allauddin approached him one day. The maestro advised him to take spiritual training from his guru. He agreed and went to Bareily with Mohammed Hussain where they met with a *sadhu* (sage). After observing Alam for a while, the holy man told his disciple Mohammed Hussain that it was no use bringing Allauddin there, as he was not after spirituality, but was interested in the *sadhana* of music. Thus, they returned.

Allauddin received training from Mohammed Hussain, who was a *beenkar* (player of the beena or Rudra Vina) of sorts. Alam went to his place at 12 noon after visiting Wazir Khan's house. Allauddin's violin performance was praised by Haidar Hussain Khan and Fida Hussain Khan, who had also come to Rampur to perform. They invited him to learn from them. Alam was also immensely benefited by Sadat Ali Khan (popularly known as Chhamman Sahib), Sahebzada, and the Home Secretary of Rampur. Allauddin received training from one Abid Ali Khan as well. (Whether this gentleman was the father of Ahmed Ali Khan – who was of the same name – remains unclear.)

He also learned many things from the Nakkals. Among these were Hiralal Nakkal, Bahadur Nakkal, Ali Afatul Nakkal, etc. Nakkals were professional imitators (impressionists) who were invited after a program featuring great musicians had been over. They were able to imitate each of the masters (that had performed at the concert) one by one.

Karim Khan, brother of renowned sitar player Hafiz Khan, imparted lessons in various types of *bandishes* and *gats* of *sitar* to Allauddin which were of immense help to him. He was also taught by one Nasir Ali Khan. Thus the favor and cooperation, received by him from all such musicians, constituted some sort of compensation to him for having missed training at the hands of Ustad Wazir Khan.

Allauddin's residing place turned into a kind of meeting ground for quite a number of musicians. They sat and smoked *hookah* (water pipe), had tea and discussed controversies and complications about musical trends and compositions. They exchanged their views in a friendly atmosphere, which was possible owing to Allauddin's great respect towards each of them. Alam listened to these valuable exchanges and he gained a good amount of knowledge from them.

WAZIR KHAN RELENTS AT LAST

Aftabuddin, Allauddin's elder brother, came to know about Allauddin's whereabouts from some confidential sources. He was informed about Nawab Hamid Ali's patronage and Wazir Khan's tutelage over his brother. Aftabuddin dispatched a telegram to Ustad Wazir Khan, requesting him to send back his brother immediately. He wrote further that Alam's wife had tried to commit suicide in his absence. She was rescued at the last moment, but everyone was afraid that her next attempt may go unnoticed and unhindered and they might not be able to save her.

The telegram had had a tremendous affect on Ustad Wazir Khan. Suddenly he remembered his solemn promise to teach Allauddin, which he had totally neglected until then. He realized his error and repented for having ignored Allauddin for such a long time.

The Ustad called his three sons – Nasir Khan, Nazir Khan and Sagir Khan (their nicknames were Piyara Mian, Majla Sahib and Chota Sahib respectively). When they arrived, he asked them about Allauddin and inquired why they had not taught him. They replied that without the Ustad's permission it had not been possible for them to impart lessons to the new disciple. They now informed their father of Alam's daily visits. Wazir Khan was deeply moved to hear all this. The Ustad called him and Allauddin arrived there trembling in fear. He showed his respect by falling flat at his feet. Wazir Khan embraced him affectionately. Tears of joy rolled down Alam's cheeks.

Wazir Khan showed Alam the telegram and inquired about his family in order to test him. Alam only touched on matters concerning his parents, brothers and sisters, but not a single word about his wife. The Ustad was surprised to see the self-restraint and madness for music on the part of the young man. But when he was asked about his married life, he meekly explained the whole story and in what circumstances he was forced to marry.

The Ustad advised him to go back to his village, but to his surprise Allauddin refused to do so. He replied that he would not show his face there until and unless he attained success in his life-long ambition. He could return there only after completing his training form Ustad Wazir Khan.

Wazir Khan was happy in seeing the young man's strong determination to reach his goal. He was astonished at the great sacrifice and trouble Allauddin had courted for the sake of music. Allauddin's patience duly impressed the Ustad. Wazir Khan now began to feel such affection for Allauddin that he asked his three sons to adopt the youth as their fourth brother. He told them to teach Alam everything they knew and promised that he would himself also train him. Wazir Khan frankly admitted his error. He told Allauddin that it was not his deliberate action, but on large part a matter of oversight or inadvertence. He further added he had forgotten about the nara ceremony itself because of his absent mindedness. But Allauddin's misfortune seemed to be over now. The Ustad made up for the loss of time by accelerating the process of his training. Wazir Khan saw the evidence of Allauddin's quickness in ascertaining material and sound musical background. He told his disciple that he would rapidly excel because of his extraordinary talent.

The Ustad told him further that he would not mind teaching him because he had now adopted Alam as his fourth son. Allauddin found no words of reply for this great man. He was astonished to notice the Ustad's affection towards him. But Allauddin remembered the vows he had taken before the *nara* ceremony and reminded the Ustad of it. He refused the Ustad's offer humbly as he did not want to disturb that particular tradition carried on by his guru. Finding him sympathetic to his traditions and practices, Wazir Khan was very pleased.

The Ustad said that he would consider Allauddin as his best disciple outside his family and he would teach him all the secrets of the art that the descendants of Tansen (one of the reputed doyens of North Indian Classical Music, who was the court musician of the Emperor Akbar) possessed. Wazir Khan was happy to know that Allauddin got his initial training from his father, who was the pupil of Ustad Kashim Ali Khan, Wazir Khan's maternal uncle.

Now the long-held ambition of the young man was realized. With his extraordinarily accurate sense of pitch, technique and musicality, Allauddin became a favorite pupil of his revered guru. Wazir Khan taught him sincerely. No one was allowed to disturb his training. Allauddin generally practiced music during the night. Allauddin's dedication was beyond human conception. The Ustad's sons also cooperated with him after seeing his enthusiasm for his subject and his immense progress.

Wazir Khan taught Allauddin dhrupad and dhamar (two branches of the form known as Dhrupad) also. He taught him the techniques and different *bajes* (styles of playing) of *beena*, *rabab* and *sursringar*, though not on the *beena* itself. Allauddin was not allowed to play *beena*, but his Ustad had explained that it would be quite possible for him to use all of the techniques and styles pertaining to *beena* on *sarod* and other instruments, and he agreed to teach him to play the *rabab* and *sursringar* – two instruments which were going out of vogue at that time.

Wazir Khan indeed kept his promise. Allauddin underwent training from this Ustad continuously for 30 years. He was taught all the secrets of Senia Gharana.

The Ustad's knowledge of his subject was colossal. One could not fathom the real depths of his knowledge. He practiced the whole night, as at that time the atmosphere would take on a highly spiritual quality. He had an attractive personality. Wazir Khan's wife was a talented *sitar* player. She sang the *Murchia* during *Muharram* (the first month of the Islamic calendar). She could sing in such an appealing way that it drew tears from the eyes of whoever listened to her. Allauddin acquired a great deal of knowledge from hearing her performances.

Ustad Wazir Khan was also loyal to a point to his patron Nawab Hamid Ali Khan. Once His Highness, the Maharaja of Kashmir came to Rampur and wanted the Ustad to be his state musician, as he was thoroughly impressed by his talent upon listening to his music. Kashmir was a bigger state than Rampur and Wazir Khan could have had many more facilities and greater comforts, but he refused the Maharaja's offer bluntly. Perhaps Allauddin was affected greatly by the strength of character of his magnanimous teacher, as he would exhibit the same strength and nobility later in his own life.

Ustad Wazir Khan was highly respected by the Nawab. His seat was even placed next to His Highness. He was given a palace to reside in and his food came from the Nawab's own cuisine. Wazir Khan was a good administrator, a good painter and a renown playwright as well. The predecessor of Nawab Hamid Ali Khan, Nawab Haidar Ali had been known to take Wazir Khan's advice in the administrative matters of his state of Rampur.

Wazir Khan considered Allauddin as his own son. He showered Alam with fatherly love and affection. Allauddin himself would behave similarly with his own students in the next phase of his life. Indeed he had imbibed all the virtuous qualities of his respected *guru*.

After completing his long training, Allauddin was ordered by his Ustad to tour different places of India and establish his own reputation, following the tradition of *diksha*, *shiksha* and *pariksha* (training, initiation and evaluation). These three features were considered the principal virtues that made one a consummate artist.

PROMINENT DISCIPLES OF USTAD WAZIR KHAN

Ustad Nasir Khan   (son)
Ustad Nazir Khan   (son)
Ustad Sagir Khan   (son)
Ustad Dabir Khan   (grandson)
Nawab Hamid Ali Khan
Nasir Ali
Abdar Rahim
Syed Ibban Ali Mian
Taraprasad Roy
Pramathnath Bandopadhya
Shrijan
Jadavendra Babu
Mohammad Hussain
Raja Nawab Ali Khan
Ustad Allauddin Khan
Ustad Hafiz Ali Khan
Pd. Vishnu Narayan Bhatkhande

The name of the doyen of the *Senia Gharana*, Ustad Wazir Khan, will live forever in splendor and glory through his eminent students and their generations. A highly successful musician, and a genius with unparalleled versatility, evidenced by mastery on various instruments, a man like Wazir Khan remains a rare personality in the history of music.

Some of the favorite *ragas* of Ustad Wazir Khan were *Darbari Kannada, Gaur Sarang, Kalyan, Todi, Mian ki Sarang*.

Allauddin Khan, blessed with extraordinary talent, enhanced his Ustad's reputation and fame by spreading Wazir Khan's immense musical treasures throughout the world, both via performance and by passing it on to his illustrious students.

Chapter 3

MASTERY IN DIFFERENT INSTRUMENTS

I T WILL BE interesting to throw light on the great skill that this versatile genius, Ustad Allauddin Khan, acquired not only in vocal music but also in a number of instruments. It is generally known that it takes a lifetime to earn complete mastery over even a single branch of music. For most masters and virtuosos, several years, covering even decades, are spent on the practice of vocal music or one particular instrument. But Ustad Allauddin possessed a prodigious ability of gaining mastery over an instrument in an uncannily short amount of time. Sometimes he assimilated the greater part of the knowledge of playing a particular instrument simply by overhearing and without direct coaching.

VOCAL MUSIC

Allauddin practiced vocal music for eight years. He could sing the 360 paltas (types of variations on patterns) and he possessed thorough knowledge about a thousand *dhrupads* and *dhamars* which he had learned from Nulo Gopal, Ustad Wazir Khan and various others. He had a vast repository of folk songs of Bengal and innumerable lighter songs based on *ragas*, including songs belonging to genres such as *bhatiali, baul*, etc.

INSTRUMENTAL MUSIC – VIOLIN

Baba first learned violin as was used in Western music from Shri Habu Dutta. Allauddin was so skilled that within a short time he could perform all of the compositions created by Shri Dutta. His violin performance had pleased band-leader Mr. Lobo Probhu of Eden Gardens. Mr. Lobo helped him to advance further in Western music through the violin. Allauddin was able to expertly read, play and write music with Western staff notation. During his stay at Rampur, he was even retained as a violin player in the orchestra of the Rampur State.

When Baba was a student of Ustad Ahmed Ali Khan, opportunities had come his way to perform as an accompanying violinist in performances given by his Ustad. On occasions, he had to give a violin recital immediately after Ahmed Ali had gone through his own program of *sarod* playing. The ovation and appreciation he received was as much as his guru.

For some time, he played violin at the court of His Highness of Patna. Here, more often than not, he had to undergo the terrible strain of playing throughout the night, non-stop or with little rest. He was, however, highly paid for his efforts.

In the days of Allauddin's bitter struggle for existence – for finding his legs as a musician, it was usually by playing violin that he could earn something, however little. He earned considerable popularity as a violinist. Allauddin was equally in his element in both solo performance and accompaniment with this favorite instrument of his early days. He became a highly favored artist of Nawab Hamid Ali Khan by the means of superb recitals on violin which he also played as an accompanist to the Nawab's vocal performances, much to the satisfaction of the Nawab. In fact, the Nawab of Rampur was so delighted with Allauddin's violin playing that he had remarked that he had had no idea that anybody in India could play this instrument with such proficiency and so brilliantly. The mastery of the violin and other instruments helped Allauddin greatly in earning favor with the great maestro Wazir Khan, and prompted the Ustad to accept Allauddin as his disciple.

Allauddin's violin pleased two other musicians of fame, Haidar Hussain Khan and Fida Hussain Khan, so much so that they themselves offered to teach Alam. Many great musicians wanted to take Allauddin on as their disciple upon hearing his violin work.

The renowned tabla player, Shri Hiru Ganguly of Calcutta wanted to perform solo in *Pancham Sawari tala* of 15 *matras* (beats), but no one dared accompany him with lehra (the time keeping melody) because of the complex nature of that particular tala-cycle. Present at the concert, Allauddin Khan immediately stood up and went to the stage. He accompanied Hiru Babu on violin, which contributed greatly to the success of the program.

In the year 1925, the Fourth All-India Music Conference held at Lucknow was one of the biggest ever of its kind. Ustad Allauddin Khan gave a magnificent display of ragas Kafi and Tilak-Kamod on violin (on January 11, 1925) with tabla accompaniment by Biru Mishra of Varanasi, who was also a *tabalchi* (tabla player) of rare competence. It so happened that in course of the splendid performance, excitement ran high both in the artists performing and the distinguished audience alike, with the two musicians striving enthusiastically to outshine and outbid each other in excellence. Allauddin's Khansaheb's performance was received with thunderous applause.

One could well imagine his skill in this instrument. An oft remembered fact was that he played his favorite instruments violin, *sarod*, *surasringar*, *rabab*, etc. left-handed, an unusual thing at that time, or, for that matter (especially, but not only, in the case of Indian instruments), for any time. Baba used to nickname the violin as *bahuleen*, which means becoming so leaned or incumbent on the arm as to lose its separate identification. Ustad Allauddin Khan did have some recordings of his violin playing.

SAROD

Allauddin Khan's very favorite instrument was the *sarod*. He was taught *sarod*, *rabab* and *surasringar* in the technique and style of *beena* (also known as *Rudra* Vina) by Wazir Khan. From his the *beenkari* (*beena* based) technique of playing, one could easily trace the source of his mastery.

Allauddin played each and every composition of Wazir Khan on sarod with great skill and beauty. Baba was a unique player of his instrument. He handled it in his own style and played it in *beenkari anga*. He became such a superb master of sarod that it became his chief instrument over the years, even though he was previously known to be master of other instruments. Allauddin Khan was reknowned as a sarod wizard. It was an unusual sight to watch him play left-handed on the instrument, a fact for which he was remembered by many.

Baba had assimilated most of the styles and techniques of Ustad Ahmed Ali, although that Ustad would avoid any advanced teaching, fearing that this over-meritorious disciple of his might outshine him in brilliance. But because of this initial sort of "self-training" by basically overhearing, Allauddin Khan had sound fundamental knowledge of the *sarod* when he began his apprenticeship with Ustad Wazir Khan. Over the years, his hard practice and knowledge helped him ultimately to evolve and develop a distinct style of his own, which earned appreciation both from great musicologists and music-lovers of India alike.

Coming out into the world at large from his training at Rampur, it was in Calcutta that he gave his first public performance. He played *sarod* in the music-conference at Bhawanipore in Calcutta. Many music stalwarts from all corners of the country had gathered there, such as Laxmi Prasad *Beenkar*, Keramatulla Khan, Emdad Khan, Vishwanath Rao, *dhrupad* singers Dani Babu and Radhika Goswami of the famous Bishnupur *gharana*. As well versed as they may have been in their lines of music, they had initially taken Allauddin for a nondescript artist and thus overlooked him. But they were in for an astonishing experience. Allauddin Khan began playing *alap*. All were spellbound and a hush fell upon the gathering of the cross-section of critics, artists, patrons and lovers of music. The mesmerized audience listened to his performance for no fewer than four hours.

In the concert, Khansaheb gave a splendid exposition of *Raga Puriya* on the sarod. Spectators were completely gripped and possessed by his rendition. Musicians of the highest status were amazed at his incontestable supremacy. Allauddin was ranked as the best musician of the conference by the panel of experts. His unparalleled triumph in this notable conference marked him out for a position of the highest level of eminence in years to come.

A player of untiring stamina, Allauddin Khan possessed exemplary mastery on sarod, an instrument which was in those days given a long berth because of the difficulty in learning it. Allauddin Khan made the sarod very popular, along with making some alterations and additions to the instrument.

In time, his fame spread throughout India. When he was retained at the Royal Court of the Maihar State and had organized his famous Maihar Band (orchestra), he took part in the fourth All India Music Conference held in Lucknow in 1925, as already noted earlier, when we touched upon his achievements there with violin. At this very place, he also gave of his best as a sarod master of the highest caliber. The famous *tabalchi*, Khalifa Abid Hussain, gave him the needed percussion accompaniment. When they reached the climax, as both of them were trying to playfully outdo the other; a marked feeling of suspense and tension developed in the course of the gripping performance, affecting both the artists and the audience. The excited masters were then requested by Pandit Vishnu Narayan Bhatkahande and Raja Nawab Ali Thakur of Lucknow to cut it short. And both acted upon the request to maintain the decency and friendly atmosphere of the conference.

The performance received wide recognition. The brilliant renditions of Ragas Gara and Darbari Kannada at the concert were talked about for some time to come. Apart from the question of trophies and financial rewards, his success at Lucknow carved out a prominent position for him as a first-class *sarod* maestro.

In 1936, Allauddin Khan earned unique distinction in Europe, particularly in Germany, playing in the presence of celebrated connoisseurs of music, who had flocked to Berlin from all over the world to see the Olympic games being held there at that time. Allauddin Khan was at this time the music director of the highly reputed orchestra in Uday Shankar's world famous dance troupe, then touring Europe.

SURSRINGAR

Allauddin Khan was equally skilled at playing the *sursringar*. His first radio-broadcasted performance on this instrument, from the Lucknow Station of All India Radio in the 1940s, instantaneously skyrocketed his fame as a *sursringari* (player of sursringar) as well. He used all the specialties of Senia Gharana in his performance. There are several rare recordings of his *sursringar* playing now preserved in the National Archives of India.

RABAB

Allauddin Khan was also known for his mastery on the *rabab*. He used the techniques from the *been* on this instrument as well, just as he did on sarod and sursringar.

He gave masterful performances of *rabab* in two sittings at the Allahabad Station of All India Radio in the year 1952. Pandit Mannulal Misra and Pandit Amarnath Misra of Varanasi accompanied him on percussion. Those performances remain regarded as historic.

HARMONIUM

The *harmonium* is a typical instrument very much in vogue throughout India. On one hand, it is considered easy to play as it is a sort of portable keyboard with a sound similar to a children's organ. It's ease of playing is partly the reason for its popularity. But to give an expert performance on harmonium is one of the hardest feats for a musician. Although many are known to be virtuosos on *sitar*, *sarod*, violin, etc., *harmonium* masters are few and far between, not as far as technique, which is relatively easy to attain on the instrument, but musical mastery, because of the limited sonic capabilities of the *harmonium*. Allauddin Khan was one of those very rare ones who could make high music on this instrument and even taught it to some pupils. However, he did not play it outside his house.

SHEHNAI

As it is known, Allauddin Khan hailed from a family of traditional *badyakars*, i.e., instrumentalist musicians especially of *shehnai* (double-reeded oboe-like instrument). His acquaintance with this wind instrument was almost hereditary. He had received long training in this instrument from his family. He played also other wind and brass instruments – clarinet, cornet, trumpet etc., and was well known for his mastery on them as well.

Ustad Allauddin Khan had enjoyed the privilege of learning *gats* from famous *sitarists* like Kallu Hafiz and Nasir Ali Khan and had heard them a great deal. But he never taught *sitar* by handling it himself, though he possessed profound knowledge about its techniques and styles.

A WELL-KNOWN PERCUSSIONIST

Baba had profound knowledge of drums such as *dhol, khol, mridanga, pakhawaj, tabla,* etc. It was his passion to acquire mastery in whichever areas of music and whichever instruments interested him.

TABLA

Allauddin was adroit in *tabla* to a high level of excellence. Once, the famous esraj player Chandrika Prasad of the *Mewa* estate (Gaya) was playing in Panch Bhairavi. The *tabla* accompaniment was provided by Shri Gagan Chatterjee, alias Bhombal, of Lucknow, but he failed to rise to the occasion and do justice to the role. Allauddin Khan, in the audience, stood up and offered his services as the percussionist and performed commendably. It turned out to be a spectacle of his mastery as a percussionist, vying with the renowned esraj player. *Larant* (dueling), *sath-sangat* (playing together) and *sawal-jawab* (question-answer) followed for hours. Everyone was taken by Allauddin's accompaniment. Among his vast number of accolades, Allauddin was awarded several gold-medals in recognition of his achievements in tabla playing as well. This earned him such a reputation that he came to be known as expert a *tabalchi* as a sarodist. It was said that whatever instrument he might be handling for the time being on any particular occasion, it invariably came to be recognized as his very best. On many occasions earlier, the young Allauddin gave *tabla* accompaniment to his *guru* Ahmed Ali Khan. In this percussion field, as well, he exhibited a good deal of originality by composing many brand-new *parans* (a particular type of rhythmic composition) in *tabla* using his unique approach.

PAKHAWAJ OR MRIDANGA

Baba was accomplished on the *mridanga* as well, also known as *pakhawaj*. His knowledge on this *Dhurpad*-based classical drum (the ancestor of the tabla) was vast.

DHOL

Allauddin Khan was an excellent *dhol*-player. Of course, he had received guidance in this instrument quite early in his life as it had been in the family line. He played *dhol* and gong with the intricate dances of Uday Shankar, the celebrated founder of the "Oriental School of Dancing." Uday Shankar later founded a Cultural

Center on the hills of Almora where Baba was invited to assume charge of the department of music as its head. During his stay at Almora as the head of this department, he taught *Bangla Dhol* (a particular type of *dhol* used only in Bengal) to the students there. Uday Shankar was highly inspired to hear *dhol* played by the Ustad. In his dance composition known as "Labor and Machinery," Shankar made plentiful use of that drum. The ballet was played in the winter of 1941 and it became a hit, or more a craze, in dance. Much of the musical credit went to Ustad Allauddin Khan, who *dhol* playing in it was landmark.

Many popular accompanists did not dare to accompany him due to his deep knowledge in almost all instruments. His mastery in so many instruments enabled him to participate in a great variety of musical soirees all over India.

Three stringed instruments of respect that he did not perform in concert were *beena*, *sitar* and *surbahar* (baritone/bass sitar) although he was acquainted with their techniques.

Chapter 4

SYSTEM OF TEACHING

USTAD ALLAUDDIN KHAN was not only a master performer but also a renowned teacher, one whose stellar accomplishments in the transmission of the art are well documented by the number of musical luminaries who studied with him and made historic marks of their own in the field of Indian Music. Allauddin Khan's approach in this area combined both the iron handed strictness of the olden times with psychological and humanist methods, the marks of modern techniques of education. The very first thing that attracted an observer's attention was his exacting and perfectionist attitude towards even the novices. He wanted his students to be seriously disposed towards their art. He also stressed obedience and devotion to the trainer or guru as a virtue of the highest order. To be a worthy student in his eyes, one had to be very hard working, intelligent and sincere. As far as Baba's own conduct towards his disciples was concerned, it was double-faceted, being both domineering and pliable.

In this respect, a kind of double personality seemed to have been developed by Ustad Allaudin Khan. On one hand, he was very modest and kind-hearted and, to a degree, honey-tongued. But at any delinquency or drawback on the part of any of his students, he would become furious and would ensure that the defaulter make reparations. It was a kind of baptism of fire that he would have his students come through. Naturally many of them could not fall in line with his arduous rules and routines, and thus they thought of leaving. The same man would again shower all his blessings upon a sincere and hard working disciple. Herein lay a kind of dichotomous aspect in Baba's character.

However, his entire attitude and approach to his disciples was characterized by his immense goodwill for their well-being and by his seemingly boundless sympathy for them in their trials and tribulations of life. Pandit Ravi Shankar, one of his most well-known disciples, has also spoken about Baba's "dual personality." In Shankar's words: "Often, he would be seated on a mat with some pillows on his hard sofa-bed, smoking a hookah, a big Indian pipe that goes hubble-bubble, when a student came in. He would say, 'Sit down. Sit down on a chair.' Now, one had to understand what he meant by that. If he was in a good mood, perhaps he really wanted the student to take the chair. But if he was in a bad temper and said, 'Oh, sit down in that chair there,' the poor unknowing student would sit down and Baba would jump up and hit him with the top of his hookah and shout, 'See! He sits on a chair right in front of me. Hah! He thinks he is my equal!' It was really very difficult to know just what Baba wanted people to do."[3]

Allauddin Khan was a hard taskmaster. He himself worked tirelessly and invariably expected the same sort of painstaking labor from his disciples. Pandit Ravi Shankar tells us: "Baba had always been a strict disciplinarian with his students, but he had imposed upon himself an even stricter code of conduct when he was a young man, often practicing sixteen to twenty hours a day, doing with very little sleep, and getting along with a minimum of material things. Sometimes, when he practiced, he tied up his long hair with a heavy cord and attached an end of the cord to a ring in the ceiling. Then, if he happened to doze while he practiced, as soon as his head nodded, a jerk on the cord would pull his hair and awaken him. From early childhood, Baba was ready and determined to make any sacrifice for music. Indeed, his entire life has been devoted to music."[4]

He was averse to all kinds of addiction. He was quick to do whatever he had on hand, never leaving it over for some other moment. His pupils were also asked to follow his example.

Students were always kept alert by their *guru's* daily routine of compactness and efficiency. The student who was agreeable to the principles and ways of life he was led by could stay there. But one that could not adjust himself to this tough atmosphere would have to leave, often in a very short time.

Initially, it was difficult to understand what Baba wanted from his disciples. But it was possible for a great many of them to become adjusted to him after some time. Of course, a majority of the music aspirants fell far short of his high standard of conduct and so had to leave empty-handed. Allauddin Khan was a teacher of the old style. He gave utmost importance to *vinaya* or humility.

Ustad Allauddin's capacity for mastering even the most intricate and difficult compositions and his subtle treatment of complex *ragas* was extraordinary. He had

---

[3]   "My Music, My Life" by Pandit Ravi Shankar.

[4]   "My Music, My Life" by Pandit Ravi Shankar.

in himself both the conceptual and the actualizing acumen. He could immediately imitate verbatim whatever he would hear. He wished of his disciples the same thing. He would have them try to develop into the same caliber. This was indeed a challenge to the students, posed deliberately by the great *guru* in order to enhance their zeal. As he went on improvising, he expected his students also to pick them up at once. He wanted them to be completely attentive to him and his superb mastery. In his own words, Baba speaks of putting his students on the alert: "As I improvise, beautiful places appear, I don't know from where. If you don't pick them up at once, they will be lost."

As A.H. Fox Strangeways in his work, "*The Music of Hindustan*," puts it: "The appearance there of one who, more than any other, may be said to personify Indian music in its broadest sense, may serve to remind us of what is surely the truth, that music does not reside in those designs and devices which can be imprisoned in symbols and committed to paper, but that it comes and goes only upon the tips of the fingers of men who are able to feel it or to create it."

This only further reiterates the unique creative power of the great master. Through his inspiring training, his talented students felt that floodgates of their own creativity had been thrown open.

Dr. Smt. Sumati Mukatkar has also paid glowing tributes to the maestro's training technique and his saintly and liberal-minded attitude to the art of music. She says, "Ustad Allauddin Khan's music was based on traditional forms. Training imparted by him acquired great traditional value and a sort of illumination. He insisted on long hours of practice. Allauddin Khan appeared to be a sort of rishi. He was a saintly person, deeply learned and affectionate. One felt that he was a person who was above any religion."

(The writer had had a dialogue with Dr. Smt. Sumati Mutatkar, in the course of which the above point was elicited.)

Baba could not tolerate mediocrity. He himself always soared around the highest pinnacle in all of his endeavors, and as such, he wanted his disciples to rise to those lofty levels of excellence, or at least strive to do so. A feeling of "remaining on top" was one of the secrets of Allauddin Khan's success as well as his students'.

Baba was known to say that the attainment of sublime resonances of music could lead one to a state of ecstasy bordering on the divine. That kind of spiritual music is believed to be only achievable by him who keeps his body, mind and soul pure. For this reason, at the beginning of training, Allauddin Khan insisted that his students lead a life of continence, signifying that they should not be addicted to sex, alcohol and materialism. This was the method of imparting training according to the ancient Indian tradition handed down from Vedic times. His students were known to have amply benefited by the following of Ustad Allauddin Khan's maxims and precepts.

Baba was conscious of the sway that music had on human psychology through its elements of melody, harmony and rhythm. His ideas in these areas are akin to the view expressed by Willard and Jones in their work, "*Music of India*." The authors state, "The power of music on the human mind has always been acknowledged to be very great, as well as its general tendency towards the soft and amiable passions."

SADHANA

The Ustad insisted that his students do intense and all-consuming practice, or *sadhana*, with full concentration of mind. Baba advised one to practice with a missionary zeal and ardent dedication to the guru and music. He said music is "*kartab vidya*." "*Kartab*" is in essence short for "*karo tab*" ("do and then . . ."), that is to say, unless one actually does something it remains undone. In this context, one of his maxims will be enlightening here. He often said, "*kare ustad na kare shagird*" (Meaning: one who "does" becomes a master, and one who "doesn't" remains a pupil.)

He asked his students to create music which would please the hearts of people and not provoke their base impulses. He always told them that during his life-long sadhana, he had felt like he was in Eternal Bliss, or Divine Rapture, three or four times. He always stressed to his students the importance of *svara sadhana* (the sadhana of the resonance and sound of the notes). According to him, *sadhana*, which means practice and discipline, eventually leads to self-realization.

Baba was also a strict follower of keeping impeccable hygiene, both personal and environmental, and he required his students to obey his views in this area of discipline. He was himself a very pious man. He always touched his instruments after his bath and namaj (prayers). He made offerings of flowers to mother Sharada – the holy wife of Shri Ramakrishna Paramhansa (he called her *Ma*), Rabindranath Tagore and Beethoven before starting his morning work. He was strictly watchful of his students in regards to whether they had bathed or not. If they had not, they were not allowed to touch any instrument. Allauddin Khan said that without proper cleanliness of mind and body one could not achieve attunement with *svaras*. The goddess of music would remain unpropitiated and they would not reach their ultimate goal. He advised them to perform their religious duties after taking a bath, and then to start practice. He enjoined upon them the *svara-sadhana* along with the continuance of practice on the instrument concerned for at least three years. His constant watch-word to his disciples was, "*Handi me nahi to chammach se kya niklega?*" ("If there is nothing in the pot, what will you serve with the ladle?" The instrument can only bring out the musical substance that is within; if there is nothing of quality inside, there is nothing of quality to play.)

Ustad Allauddin Khan attached a large amount of importance to vocal music. According to our classical tradition, instrumentalists are required to have a moderate command over the voice right from the start, because the foundation of Indian music is vocal. It is composed primarily of melody, embellishment, and rhythm. Any melodic phrase, with or without a definite rhythm, that can be tuned vocally must also be played on an instrument (as much as possible), with each instrument's own features introducing a special quality to the sound.

Baba started with *sargam* (solfeggio) and *palta* (variations of note patterns) which were followed by *gats* (fixed compositions). He imparted thorough training in *meend* (glissandi), *gamak* (rapid, repeated and accurate glissandi from one note to another and back), different types of *taans* (linear movements of musical material), *jhala* (percussive climax), *krintan* (pull-offs and hammer-ons), *sparsa* (grace notes) and *murchhana* (scale modulations). These are considered to comprise the foundation of *svara-sadhana* and indispensable for carefully delincating the *raga* and its distinctive notes and phrases, and correctly using the microtones, or *srutis*, to convey the proper effect of the *raga* and make the music come alive.

Ustad Allauddin Khan recommended the practice at dawn to start with *Raga Bhairav* and stressed on *Gaur Sarang* as a *raga* appropriate to practice at noontime. He preferred *Yaman* as the best evening exercise, while prescribing *Kafi* to be sung by a pupil who was in between two different *thats* (parent scales) associated with specified *ragas*. This sequence of practice, perhaps with a little variation here and there, was studied thoroughly for years. This study was also accompanied by the practice of rhythmic figures through the use of specific right-hand (plucking hand) strokes, such as da (up), ra (down), diri (double stroke) and their various combinations.

Thus it was for the fundamentals. The secondary phase was equally arduous, although often spiced with moments of great musical explorations. Allauddin Khan insisted on the reproduction of his compositions by hearing them as a matter of course. He assessed the depth of knowledge of his students through the above process.

Baba corrected the minor mistakes without much admonishment, but adopted a stern attitude to faults of a major type. Thus the students acquired the sense of correct assessment of *sruti, chalan, vadi, samvadi* (elements of *ragas*) etc.

He taught *laya* (tempo work) along with *gatkari* (use of a composition with variation and improvisation relating to that composition). To help this, a student had to also undergo at least preliminary training in *tabla* and *pakhawaj* as well. They were required to play the drums in the presence of the Ustad, so that they could learn how to master *laya* (meaning, in this case, polyrhythmic skill) which covered *deri, ari, sawari, jhulna, pipilika, sam, visham, ati, anaghat*, etc. (aspects of rhythm, tempo and polyrhythms).

Allauddin Khan taught *gats* (fixed compositions which one uses as a stable pole in the improvisations) composed in *trital* (a cycle of 16 beats, also known as *tintal*) at first. Gradually the students had to pick up *gats* composed in different *talas*, such as *dhamar* (14 beats) *jhaptal* (10 beats) etc. He imparted to them the proper training of *taan, tora, layakari* (linear and rhythmic figures) etc., along with the *gats*. Sometimes, Baba himself played *tabla* and his students had to practice *larant* (phrases against the cycle) to his *sangat* (accompaniment) and, more often than not, this *guru-sisya* duo would go on for hours on end.

While mastering the rudiments of music, the student learned all of the techniques necessary to properly handle the instrument of his choice. This he did by working in a particular idiom, tonal range and artistic scope of a given instrument by practicing scales, *paltas*, *sargams* and *bols* (syllabic patterns) taught by the *guru*. The Ustad first gave many pieces of fixed music in the form of *gats* and *taans* (musical lines – composed in the beginning stages of learning, and later improvised) based on a particular *raga*. Fixed compositions in particular are called *bandishes*, which literally means "bound." But in this context it means well engraved. These are vocal or instrumental pieces, either traditionally handed down as they had been for generations, or the teacher's own creations. Students learned and memorized these by playing the same material over hundreds and even thousands of times, to be able to produce the correct and most precise sound, intonation and phrasing. Thus, Baba helped lay down a solid foundation of technique as well as sound knowledge of the *ragas* and *talas* for the benefit of the student for all of his/her career.

Baba took up the teaching of *alap* in the final phase of training. *Alap* (the opening of the presentation of a *raga*, where the *raga* being played is exposed slowly, note by note, without rhythmic accompaniment) received the utmost importance at his hands. While imparting training in this line, he led the students carefully, as one inadvertent turn of phrase could ruin the specific mood supposed to be elicited by a particular *raga*, thereby possibly leaving a blemish in the performance, so easily perceived by the audience in this most exposed of the sections of a presentation.

The traditional classification of thematic content in Indian arts is embodied in the *nava rasas* (the nine sentiments of classical Indian philosophy and aesthetics). *Sringar* (the play of opposites, love, erotic), *Hasya* (comic), *Karuna* (tenderness, pathos and compassion), *Raudra* (fiery or anger), *Vira* (heroic or noble), *Bhayanak* (horrifying or fright), *Vibhatsa* (disgusting or gruesome), *Adbhuta* (astonishing or incredible), and *Shanta* (tranquil or peace). But from Allauddin Khan's point of view of aesthetic he considered three amongst these to be the most important in a musical performance of Indian Classical Music, namely, *Karuna* (pathos), *Sringar* (love and erotic) and *Vira* (valor) as the basic sentiments that gave rise to the rest as their ramifications. Following this conceptualization, he concluded that *alap* (in this case – the part with no apparent pulse, or the first section of the larger whole section known as "*Alap*") was the embodiment of *Karuna* (tenderness, pathos and compassion). As the Alap as a whole rises higher and higher to its climax, the other two predominant *rasas* or sentiments – *Sringar* and *Vira* – automatically follow in the shape of *jod* (second section of *alap* with a pulse but still without percussion) and *jhala* (the rhythmic climax of the *alap* – but still without the entrance of percussion instruments).

If Allauddin Khan found any of his disciples capable of playing solo because of his or her exceptional talent, he helped develop his creative faculty further in various ways. Baba encouraged his students to improvise when they reached advanced stages, as is necessary to ultimately play *ragas* properly on the professional stage.

It is believed that the right temperament of a *raga* is something that must be infused by the *guru* in the consciousness of the disciple, and it was up to the disciple to cultivate the basic seed into a luxuriant plant of musical sensitivity. Unlike some other musicians, Baba never withheld musical material nor did he have any jealous mental reservations about passing on to deserving students the great and sacred knowledge, as well as the grasp of the sublime and ecstatic art he had mastered.

Baba's teaching was unique and exemplary. His compositions or bandishes always tended to be spiritual rather than erotic. An example of such a bandish is noted below: –

"Hey kanhaiya hil mil ke bisar na jaiyo"

(Meaning:"O Lord Krishna, after showing such great affection, do not forget me.")

According to him, one could not learn music only by reading a book or by overfeeding oneself with notation only. He believed that the *guru-sishya parampara* (guru-disciple lineage) was the ideal way to learn the art.

Baba did not allow his disciples to note down anything. He urged upon them the need to assimilate and memorize whatever lessons and illustrations were being taught to them in order that the inner connection to music would be permanent and real.

Ustad Allauddin was strictly against the conferment of any degree whatsoever. Baba used to say that people were more after degrees than the art itself. At the same time, when it came to the subject of degrees in general, he was in support of the offering of degrees to women. He believed in equal education for both sexes and not have the paper documents of proof of education be distributed only to men.

Allauddin Khan held strongly to the philosophy of painstaking exertion to attain fulfillment of one's mission in any sphere. As Baba used to say, one should do hard labor in one's most favorite *anga* (aspect) so as to get perfectly skilled in it; this was the first thing. Following this process, one could master all the other *angas* as well in subsequent phases.

BABA'S PRACTICAL WAY OF TEACHING

Ustad Allauddin's practical training was rigid and orthodox in certain aspects. He stressed that one should take training in *sargams* (solfeggio) for not less than five years, during which they had to learn *sur-mantra, palta, murchhana, bol, sapat-tan, lari-tan, jhala, krintan*, etc. (different elements of note application). A few glimpses of the above techniques are depicted in the following lines.

Sur-mantra (incantations connected to the solfeggio)

This may be termed as Baba's own peculiar style of teaching which was aimed at including a perfect sense of svara and lava. For example: –

PG PARE SADHU SHARANANA DHARE DHYANA

PG PR   SD   SRṆṆ   ḌR   DṆ

RAMA SHYAMA MADHU NAM SWARUP

RM   SM   MD   NM   SRP

GIRIDHARI OM

GRDPR   SṆ-S

Palta (methodical variations of patterns)

Ustad Allauddin laid great emphasis on doing *palta* which was used as the basis of a musician's performance. He devised several types of it, using different note combinations. One example is given below with *arohana* (ascent) and *avarohana* (descent):

Arohana: SRG SRGM, RGM RGMP, GMP GMPD, MPD MPDN, PDN PDNṠ

Avarohana: ṠND ṠNDP, NDP NDPM, DPM DPMG, PMG PMGR, MGR MGRS

Baba also formulated a series of exercises in which *paltas* were prescribed for practice in three octaves.

Murchhana (scale modulation)

This was one of the areas which the Ustad stressed greatly. Much like the "white-key" modulation in Western music, the range of a scale is played from different starting points, ending in the octave of the starting note. Such as from S to S, N to N and so on. They again come back from *mandra saptak* (lower octave) to the *madhya saptak* (middle octave):

Arohana: S R G M P D N Ṡ

Avarohana: Ṡ N D P M G R S

(Editor's note: The starting point changes with every repetition. The next ascent would begin with R and continue to its octave above.*)*

He prescribed the practice in three octaves, which means playing *sargams* in three octaves — *mandra* (low), *madhya* (middle), and *tara* (high) saptaks (octaves). Some

Arohana: Ṇ S R G M P D N

Avarohana: N D P M G R S Ṇ

of the *murchhanas* are reproduced below:

Arohana: Ṣ Ṛ G̣ M P̣ Ḍ Ṇ S

Avarohana: S Ṇ Ḍ P̣ M G̣ Ṛ Ṣ

Arohana: Ṛ G̣ M P̣ Ḍ Ṇ Ṣ Ṛ

(and back and so on from different starting points in all octaves)

(Editor's note: It must be understood that these are only the first stages of the exercises. The technical development required for this music is of the highest levels in the world and is beyond the scope of this book to convey more than these basic examples of the starting points.)

Let it be noted here that there was no hard and fast limit to the passage of the notes over the different *saptaks*, as far as Baba was concerned. His melodic canvas embraced roaming even in *ati-mandra* (two octaves below middle octave) and *tara* (upper) *saptaks* (octaves). But it provided a solid foundation for students. It was a tremendous task to play all these *murchhanas* in all of the octaves without stopping.

Bols (rhythmic syllables of the right/plucking hand)

Ustad Allauddin Khan taught his disciples to pay utmost attention and devote immense labor to *bols*. It formed a special feature of his unique style. As we have stressed earlier, Baba embodied in himself a rare synthesis of the most subtle nuances of different instruments. This extraordinary synthesizing acumen enabled the Ustad to apply *bols* (rhythmic syllables connected with right hand strokes) of the *sarod* to other instruments as well, and vice-versa.

He taught the technique and variations of the fundamental bols *da* (downstroke symbolized by "|") *ra* (upstroke symbolized by "0") and *diri* (double stroke – up and down in rapid succession – symbolized by "v") and innumerable combinations of the three at different tempos. The practice of bols was very specific: – First, sixteen times of each of the *bols*, then eight times of the same and after that four times. All these had to be done with every note of every scale in ascending and descending orders.

It is easy to see that the constant practice of these very finely conceived sequences of *bols* would help students to set their fingers and hands and even their entire physical system to become attuned to the various aspects of playing their instruments. Baba's treatment of the *bols* and, for that matter, many other musical devices, was analytical. As he liked to make galaxies of all possible and conceivable combinations of these, he also laid stress on their single and individual handling. Thus he also gave patterns on the following lines:

Arohana: S̶ R̶ G̶ M̶ P̶ D̶ N̶ Ṡ̶

Avarohana: Ṡ̶ N̶ D̶ P̶ M̶ G̶ R̶ S̶

Arohana: S₀ R₀ G₀ M₀ P₀ D₀ N₀ Ṡ₀

Avarohana: Ṡ₀ N₀ D₀ P₀ M₀ G₀ R₀ S₀

(The significance here is that the right hand strokes are different in the two ascents and descents.)

(Editor's note: It must be understood that these are only the first stages of the exercises. The technical development required for this music is of the highest levels in the world and is beyond the scope of this book to convey more than these basic examples of the starting points.)

Taan

Ustad Allauddin advised his pupils to be give careful attention towards *taans* (lines of musical material), of which he taught many kinds. A few of them have been given below:

Ekhara Taan

```
DN  SR  GR  SR        RG  MP  DP  MP

lo  lo  lo  lo        lo  lo  lo  lo
x                     2


DN  ṠṚ  ĠṚ  ṠṚ        ṠN  DP  MG  RS

lo  lo  lo  lo        lo  lo  lo  lo
0                     3
```

Sapat Taan *(line covering a large range of the instrument, and moving in a non-circuitous, or straight motion; only the basic idea is shown here; the notes in actuality must conform to the rules of the particular Raga)*

Baba said that *sapat taans* should be practiced so much that even high speeds each of its notes should be clear and accurate.

```
G  Ṃ  P  Ḍ  N  S  R  G  M  P  D  N  Ṡ  Ṛ  Ġ  Ṁ

I  o  I  o   I  o  I  o   I  o  I  o   I  o  I  o
x         2          0          3


Ṗ  Ṁ  Ġ  Ṛ  Ṡ  N  D  P  M  G  R  S  N  Ḍ  Ṗ  Ṃ

I  o  I  o   I  o  I  o   I  o  I  o   I  o  I  o
x         2          0          3
```

Sparsha (touching other tones for resonance)

This aspect of melody is to add to the effect of a particular note by ringing up sympathetic sounds from some other selected ones.

Arohana: S R   R G   G M   M P   P D   D N   N Ṡ

Avarohana: Ṡ N   N D   D P   P M   and so on.

(Editor's note: It must be understood that these are only the first stages of the exercises. The technical development required for this music is of the highest levels in the world and is beyond the scope of this book to convey more than these basic examples of the starting points.)

Krintan (embellishment by a means of pulling off and quickly hammering on notes)

Allauddin Khan had a great liking for this beautiful way of ornamentation.

/RS - ṆS\   /GR - SR\   /MG - RG\   /PM - GM\

/DP - MP\   /ND - PD\   /ṠN - DN\

Sargam (structures in solfeggio)

With the help of *sargam*, a student gets a fair idea of a *raga* in a simple profile. Baba insisted on his students practicing sargam in *tala* so that they could also develop sufficient knowledge of *laya* simultaneously. A *sargam* of *Raga Yaman-Kalyan* is given here:

Raga Yaman Kalyan Tala: Tritaal (Tintaal – 16 beats) Time: Evening

Sthai

N D P M	G R G M	N D M-	P M G R
0	3	x	2

G M P M	G R S N	D N - M	- D N R
0	3	x	2

G R G M	P D N D	P M G M	G R S -
0	3	x	2

Antara

N D P M	G R G M	S R G S	R G M P
0	3	x	2

D N Ṡ N	D P M G	R G M P	D N Ṙ -
0	3	x	2

D - Ġ Ṙ	- D - Ṙ	Ṡ N D P	M P N D
0	3	x	2

P M G M	G R S N	D N - M	- D N R
0	3	x	2

G R G M	P D N D	P M G M	G R S -
0	3	x	2

Baba had said that the above *svaragram* (*sargam*) was composed by Ustad Bahadur Hussain Khan.

(*This sargam was learned from Shri Rebati Ranjan Debnath, who had received it from Baba himself.*)

Gamak (rapid and repeated portamenti)

Baba taught various types of *gamaks*. Chief characteristics of his *gamak* formulations were their tonal purity and sublime temperament. These were aimed more at creating an environment of gravity in our enjoyment of the various *rasas*.

Arohana: S R R̄ G R G R S, R G Ḡ M G M G R

G M M̄ P M P M G, M P P̄ D P D P M

P D D̄ N D N D P, D N N̄ S̄ N S̄ N D

Avarohana: D N N̄ S̄ N S̄ N D P D D̄ N D N D P

and so on

Meend or sut (glissandi)

Ustad Allauddin Khan's designed practice for developing the technique of one of the finest of musical devices known as *sut* or *meend* (glissandi or the musical gliding between notes with perfect intonation) served two purposes. These were:

(i) kindling in the mind of the novice an accurate sense of intonation, and enable him to understand such, and

(ii) grasp a single note as a culmination of a series of preceding pitches of sound.

Arohana: SRS RGR GMG MPM PDP DND

NṠN

Avarohana: NṠN DND   and so on

In the subsequent phase of teaching, Baba taught different *gats* (instrumental compositions) in various *ragas* (also in different *talas*) appropriate to particular periods of time in the span of a day. Thus the dawn *Raga Bhairav* and the *ragas* associated with it were selected for practice during the morning hours. In the same way one or two other *ragas* such as "*Yaman* and "*Bhupali*" were practiced in the evening using different *gats*. A *gat* contained different types of *taans* (lines) and *jhalas* (climactic movements).

Masitkhani gat (gat usually played in slow tempos (but not always) and with very specific rhythmic restrictions)

Raga Yaman (Vilambit – slow) Tala: Tritaal (Tintaal – 16 beats) Time: Evening

Sthai

```
GG |R SS N R |G G G RR |G MM P M |G R S
 v | I  v  I o | I  I  o  v | I  v  I o | I  I  o
   |3          |x          |2         |0
```

```
GG |R SS N D |N D P MM |D NN R G |G R S
 v | I  v  I o | I  I  o  v | I  v  I o | I  I  o
   |3          |x          |2         |0
```

Antara

```
PP |M GG M D |N Ṡ Ṡ ṠN |Ṡ ĠṘ Ġ Ṁ |Ġ Ṙ Ṡ
 v | I  v  I o | I  I  o  v | I  v  I o | I  I  o
   |3          |x          |2         |0
```

```
ṠṠ |N DD N Ṙ |N D P PP |M GG R G |G R S
 v | I  v  I o | I  I  o  v | I  v  I o | I  I  o
   |3          |x          |2         |0
```

Raga Yaman (Drut – fast) Tala: Tritaal Time: Evening

```
                    |              |
S GG R G | - G - M | P - P M | G R S N
 I  v  I  o    - I - o    I - I o    I o I o
0            3          x          2


N D NN SS | N ND -D P | M PP M D | - D N S
 I  o  v v    I- oI  -o I    I  v  I  o   -  I I o
0             3            x          2


          |            |
N S - G | R N - R | P - P M | G R S N
 I o - I   o I - o    I - I o    I o I o
0          3          x          2
```

Baba often composed his own lyrics for his compositions. He also sang many songs whose music was composed by his elder brother Aftabuddin Gunakar, as well as many other compositions of *baul* and *bhatiali* (Bengali folk-music genres) which were often based on certain *ragas*. When he sang them he directed his trainees to copy him verbatim, like an impression through carbon paper, to the best of their respective capacities. They were required to follow him both vocally and instrumentally.

Here is one of Baba's most beloved songs, the music of which was composed by his elder brother Aftabuddin:

Raga: Jhinjhoti Tala: Jhap (10 beats) Time: Evening

S N̲	S R S	- N̲	D̲N̲ Ḍ Ṗ
Shi kha	e de tui	a -	ma - re -
x	2	0	3

Ḍ Ḍ	- S S	- R	M G M
Ke mon	ko - re	to -	re da ki
x	2	0	3

- -	- - -	R -	M M M
		E k	da ke tui
x	2	0	3

- R	M M M	P M	G -G M
- fu	ri e de	re -	Jo - n -mo
x	2	0	3

RG S	- R G	M G	- - -
bho ra	- da ka	da ki	
x	2	0	3

Raga Pahari was one of Baba's favorites. A *drut* (fast) *gat* composed by him is cited below:

Raga Pahari Tala: Tritaal (16 beats) Time: Evening

```
NN DD | P DD M G | - S - R | M - - M | G R
 v  v |  |  v  | o | - | - o | | - - | | | o
      |  0        |  3      |x        |2

NN DD | P DD M G | - S - R | M - - G | R G
 v  v |  |  v  | o | - | - o | | - - | | | o
      |  0        |  3      |x        |2

S - | - S R N | D P - D | M PP M PP | D SS
| - | - | | o | | | - o | | v | v | | v
     | 0       | 3       |x           |2

R G | S RR M P | D S - N | D P - M | G -
| o | | v | o | | | - o | | | - o | | -
     | 0       | 3       |x        |2
```

Ustad Allauddin had a great fondness for *Raga Tilak-Kamod*. He said that *Tilak-Kamod* was a specialty of Rampur. His *guru*, Ustad Wazir Khan Sahib, composed a slow *gat* which was very dear to the Nawab of Rampur. The name of the particular *gat* was *Huzur Pasand*.

In Baba's Maihar Band, the following drut gat of *Tilak-Kamod* was performed.

Raga: Tilak-Kamod Tala: Tritaal (16 beats) Time: Evening

```
P NN S R  | - G  R G | S - M - | G R S N
I  v  I o | -  I - I o| I - I - | I o I o
0           3           x         2

R MM M P | - Ṡ N Ṡ | P D P M | G S - N
I  v  I o| -  I I o| I o I o | I I - o
0          3          x        2

P - P S  | - S R R | R G RR MM | G S - N
I   o I  | - o I o | I o  v  v | I I - o
0          3         x           2

S RR S R | R GG R G | M P GG MM | G S - N
I  v  I o| I  v  I o| I o v   v | I I - o
0          3           x          2

S RR M P | Ṡ - P D | - M G - | G S - N
I  v  I o| I - I o | - I o - | I I - o
0          3          x        2
```

Ustad Allauddin Khan equally liked to play and sing *Bengali kirtans** (Bengali devotional songs) and *Palli-gitis* (village songs). One of his favorite *kirtan* songs was –

*"Man re pagal
Hare Krishna bol
Hoyo na chanchal
Bhava sagare."*

(Meaning: Oh crazy Mind! Say "Hare Krishna" (Glory to the Lord). Do not be restless in the sea of the world.)

(Editor's note: This type of "kirtan" is only prevalent in the province of Bengal and is NOT at all the same as the chant-oriented "kirtan" that is prevalent throughout the devotional circles of India (also sung by Westerners today). The Bengali kirtan is poetic and is often accompanied by folk theater depicting scenes of devotion to the Lord in His different incarnations.)

A specimen of his *palli-giti* or village folk song is also given here –

*"Man majhi tor bhaitha ne re toole
Ami ar baite pari na."*

(Meaning: Oh mind, my boatman! Take up the rowing-staff – I cannot row any longer.)[5]

ALAP

This was the final phase of training that was chalked out by the great maestro for his wards. Baba used to teach *alap*, spread over various stages of tonal development, arranged in a gradually undulating tenor and tempo. Allauddin Khan emphatically laid down that *alap* should begin with a devotional mental frame, deeply absorbed in the contemplation of a selfless or "super-self" reality, as manifest in the words – *Ananta Hari Om* (The Infinite Supreme Reality).

In general, there are three types of *alap.*

(i)   *raga alap*
(ii) *rupak alap*
(iii) *aochar-anga alap*

---

[5]   This was one of Baba's favorite songs and he was often heard humming it to himself, even until the end of his years. The late Shri Rebati Ranjan Debnath was told about it by Baba's daughter-in-law Zubeda Khatoon (the first Mrs. Ali Akbar Khan) when Shri Debnath was at Maihar immediately after the master's death.

For the purpose of initiating his students in the *raga* a*lap* (which is the "classic *alap*" in its full form), Baba divided this aspect of the art into several sections, keeping with the temperament and peculiarities of a *raga*.

It is worth mentioning here that Baba's *taans* (lines of musical substance, adhering to a *raga*) in the style of *Khayal* (the most prevalent form of North Indian Classical Music) were taught to his students instrumental music in *svaragram* and tonal articulation, just as in the case of vocal music. Another characteristic of his skillful teaching in instrumental music was that he insisted on his students' singing the *gats*, *taans*, etc., alongside playing them instrumentally.

Baba also taught his students to sing *taranas* (syllabic vocal pieces in a fast tempo) along with their instrument playing. He taught many *bandishes* (compositions) based on *taranas*.

He also imparted practical training in percussion instruments like *tabla*, *pakhawaj*, etc. to all his pupils learning non-percussion instruments. He had all of them master a large number of compositions for percussion instruments.

BABA'S ROUTINE PRACTICE

Allauddin Khan's practice system commenced with *sargams* followed by one *jhala* each, so that the fingering of the left hand could be perfected. Then came the phase of playing only *sargams* in three scales. Hereafter *bols*, *ragmalika* (sequence of *ragas* strung together like a garland) and *gat* would have to be gone through successively one after another. He insisted on playing the *Masitkhani gat* as slowly as possible and beautifying it with various phrases.

Ustad Allauddin Khan (1881–1972)

Allauddin Khan with Timir Baran – 1920s

Allauddin Khan's well-known Maihar band
The Report of the 4th All-India Music Conference, Lucknow 1925

Allauddin Khan, Jamaluddin Khan, Abid Hussain, Hafiz Ali Khan

*Hirendrakumar Ganguly, Aashish Khan, Allauddin Khan
Ali Akbar Khan, & Ravi Shankar*

Allauddin Khan's Home

Allauddin Khan playing Rabab

Allauddin Khan reprimands an erring musician with his cane at a concert given in his honor by the Maihar band, 1968

Ravi Shankar, Allauddin Khan and Ali Akbar Khan

Allauddin Khan, Ali Akbar Khan
Aashish Khan

Ali Akbar Khan, Vilayat Khan
Kesarbai Kerkar, Allauddin Khan
Kanthe Maharaj, 1952

Music Conference
President Rajendra Prasad - Delhi, 1952

Samta Prasad, Ravi Shankar, Allauddin Khan, Ali Akbar Khan

Vasant Rai, Ravi Shankar, Allauddin Khan, Ali Akbar Khan

Bade Ghulam Ali Khan with Allauddin Khan

Allauddin Khan enjoying fish

Allauddin Khan playing violin

Allauddin Khan, Ravi Shankar and Gyan Prakash Ghosh

Allauddin Khan and Gyan Prakash Ghosh

Ali Akbar Khan

Ravi Shankar

Annapurna Devi

Sharan Rani

Ashish Khan

Pannalal Ghosh

Nikhil Banerjee

Wazir Ali Khan

Timir Baran

Annapurna Devi

Kanthe Maharaj, Allauddin Khan
Kishan Maharaj

* Photostat copy of Ustad Allauddin Khan's letter of 9.6.57,
  written from Maihar to Shri Rebati Ranjan Debnath.

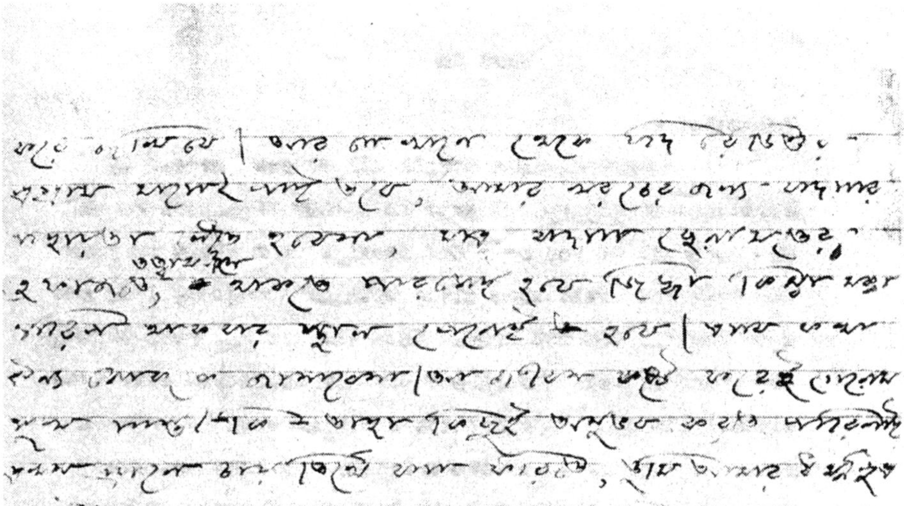

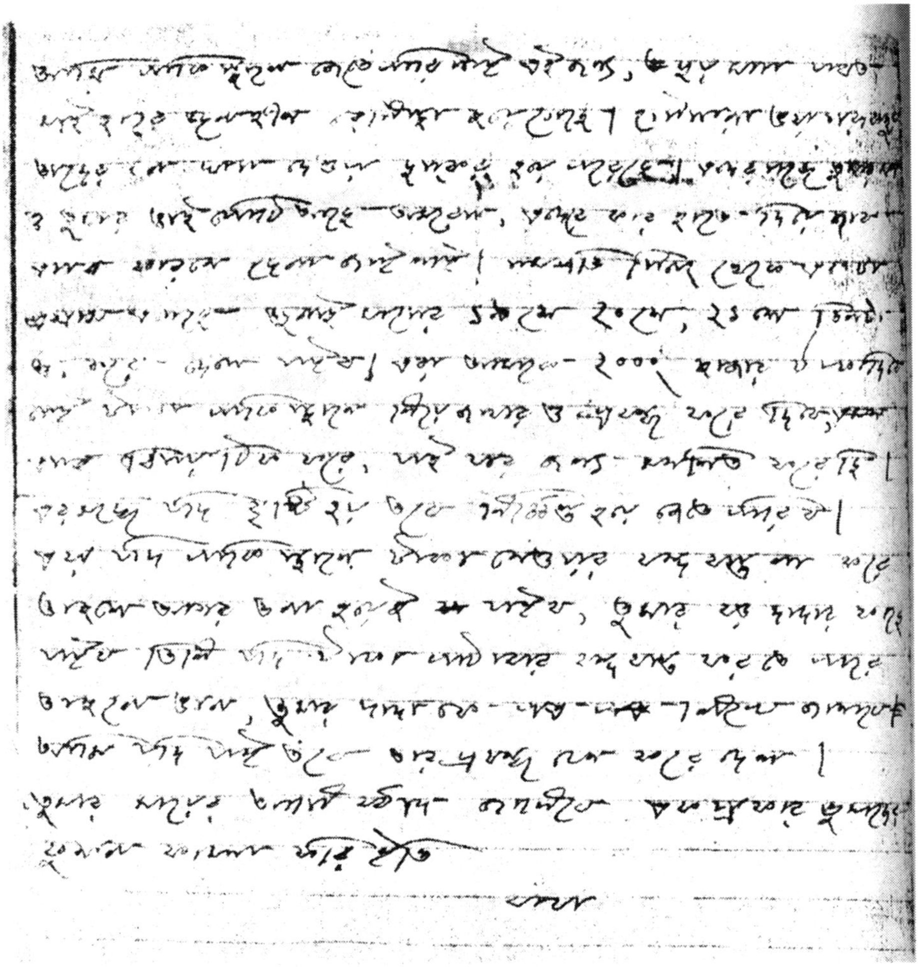

Chapter 5

VAST ACHIEVEMENTS

NOT ONLY DID Ustad Allauddin Khan attain great success in the field of music, but he excelled in almost all aspects of life. He was a great musician, a model teacher, a saintly person and an enthusiastic social reformer. Noble-souled, he was a man of character and rectitude. Although with a spiritual and philosophical bent of mind, he did not evince any nonchalance to those traits of human conduct that help and enhance a person's material life as well. He was punctual and precise to a fault. At the same time, he never failed to show a taste for humor even in the midst of his sternness as a teacher.

Moreover, he was a patriot, cherishing a deep sympathy for his apathy-filled, enslaved countrymen when they gasped under the boots of foreign imperialism. After the independence of India, he never ceased to look forward to a bright future of prosperity and glory for the motherland and her countless sons and daughters.

Perhaps his only weak point, if it can be at all termed so, was his quick temper. Still, it cannot be said that his irritability was meant to create malice between himself and anybody else. What he cared for, when he became furious, was that a certain thing was not done in a proper way or that a particular fault or indiscretion on somebody's part needed to be corrected. One mitigating factor regarding his excessive ire was that it vanished as quickly as it possessed his being, leaving no trace whatsoever either in his subsequent dealings.

Although man of genius and considerable and innumerable achievements, he never gave way to conceit or arrogance. It is interesting to know his own estimations about his accomplishments. Doubtless, his knowledge in the different branches of music – vocal and instrumental – was encyclopedic. However, in his modesty, he often said, "My knowledge is like a drop in a vast ocean of promise."

Another noticeable feature was that he was not catapulted to the loftiest summit overnight. He had to build the edifice of his glory and fame brick by brick. The one constant factor in his hard struggle was that he was never taken over by disappointment and despair enough to give up his objective and endeavors as lost. On the contrary, he strode forward with steady steps, although sometimes slowly.

About his achievement it may be accurately said that he paid for them with his blood and sweat, as it were. But as the journey of most great persons, Baba's perseverance and determination did win out, and in scores.

Uthaistha jagratha prappaya baran nibodhata
Shurasaya dhara nishita durotaya
Doorga pathastat kavayo badanti.

(Meaning: Arise, awake, and realize the blessings that are due to you. Great thinkers say that the road is difficult like the edge of a razor.)

AS A MUSICIAN

In India there are many saints and *yogis* who have renounced their families, relatives, wealth and comforts for the wake of their spiritual pursuits. They move from place to place in search of their objective. They search for a competent *guru* who can guide them along their spiritual path. For this purpose they visit various religious places in different states, dwelling amongst many pious souls. At the same time, there also exists another category of people who believe that they can achieve the same spiritual fulfillment through the medium of music. They worship God through music. They leave behind all they possess to quench their thirst with the art. They are madly in love with music. They also wander to whatever places necessary to find the right type of teacher who can open their eyes to catch the celestial beauty of the realm of music. More often than not, they undergo a great deal of hardships and difficulties. Ustad Allauddin Khan of Maihar acquired his huge stock of musical wealth along the rough path of penury, starvation and untold hardships. Like truth itself, the story of his life sounds stranger than fiction. He was one who achieved his spiritual goal through music.

Baba's talent in music had been obvious from the very beginning, but adverse circumstances put many obstacles in his way. Through his firm determination he overcame them all and continued his great mission of securing North Indian Classical Music its rightful place, its wisdom practically lost through ignorance and misuse (except to a handful of rare masters). His whole life was one of selfless dedication to the service of the Muses.

During the last 100 years, two names have dominated the realm of *sarod* in Indian instrumental music: Ustad Allauddin Khan of Maihar and Ustad Hafiz Ali Khan of Gwalior. These two eminent masters were like two streams flowing out of the same source, as the preceptor for both was the celebrated and incomparable Ustad Wazir Khan of Rampur.

Allauddin Khan did a great deal to elevate the art of music to a higher level in common society. In the area of its research and experimentation, he can be mentioned as a pioneer along with luminaries such as Pandit Vishnu Digambar Paluskar. As already mentioned in the previous pages, he spared no pains to free music from the clutches of those who would misuse the art, including the orthodox Ustads, whose die-hard conservative attitudes brought about stagnation in the natural flow of musical progress, keeping it as a close preserve for a few individuals. It is not improper to state that his efforts served to build a bridge between Indian Classical Music and the common people.

Today, the names of two prominent artists come to the forefront regarding Ustad Allauddin Khan: his son (the late) Ustad Ali Akbar Khan (*sarod*) and his son-in-law Pandit Ravi Shankar (*sitar*), both of whom have enjoyed international fame and respect. They are known to have been the most outstanding exponents of the innovations and specialties introduced in the treatment of a good many *ragas* by Baba, whether simply as variations or with substantial, even radical, departures from the orthodox rules. Allauddin Khan was among those very few Ustads who had shed the traditional bias of keeping their wealth of musical wisdom as a family treasure. He generously distributed his knowledge to whoever cared to receive it.

Baba achieved unique distinction in the field of music as a vocalist and instrumentalist. But as he was not keen to give performances in public as a vocal musician, this side of his musical genius remained rather shrouded as far as the world of music lovers was concerned. Since he preferred to appear before the public eye as an instrumentalist only, very little remained on record about his achievements in vocal music.

He was one of the first to break free of the shackles set by stereotyped ways of dealing with any particular *raga*. He led his disciples away from the sectarian and restricted views then prevailing in the sphere of Indian music during the first quarter of the 20th century.

We may talk of generalists and specialists in the field of music like any other area of human learning and skill. In the accepted sense, a generalist, although highly proficient in a large number of aspects of the particular branch of learning, may fall short of the standard of a specialist in a single specific branch. But in the case of Allauddin Khan this stereotype did not hold. Having command over all branches of Indian music – vocally and instrumentally, he was certainly a generalist. Even in the area of instruments itself he was a generalist, as he had mastered several instruments almost to an equal degree. At the the same time due to his sophisticated and highest level of knowledge and skill in the minutest aspects of an instrument, he became even something more than a specialist in it. His "specialization" (for lack of a better term) encompassed a wide range of instruments. It was a rare feat for any single individual, however talented, to have achieved the highest degree of mastery in so many branches of music within a single lifetime. Not only could he provide an almost boundless repertoire of both vocal and instrumental forms – such as *alap*, *dhrupad-dhamar*, *khayal*, *tarana*, *tappa*, *thumri* – but he could synthesize them, so as to create an entirely new and wholistic concept of performance and interpretation of music.

Baba initiated an altogether original style. This style was the outcome of his deep insight into the various aspects of music and his creative genius which not only churned the best from the celebrated *gharanas* of his *gurus* but developed these traditions further and to such a depth and magnitude that the resultant fruit became something brand new and, one can say, different from the achievements of the forerunners. Although his original creations bore all the marks of genuine art in complete agreement with theoretical tenets, he had to face adverse criticism. He was labeled as an "impurist." Pandit Ravi Shankar has said, "Baba faced much criticism in the beginning, as indeed, some of us, as his disciples, have been and are still facing. Early in his career, he was reproached for not playing pure sarod when he performed and was criticized for bringing other techniques into his playing."[6]

The crux of the matter was that Baba had been such a powerful and intelligent force in not only one single branch of music or, for that matter, in one single instrument, but in several branches and instruments, that effects of being involved in the different aspects could not but be manifest in his music, whatever might be its momentary instrumental vehicle. Shri Jotin Bhattacharya put it in this way, "He had derived the essence of each baz (style), each pattern, and blended them into a musical rainbow." Can this be branded as "impure" simply because it is original?

These critics seemed to miss sight of the fact that for him compartmentalization of any particular instrument or any particular aspect of music was unthinkable. Boundaries and limitations circumscribing an instrument or a single aspect of music lost their boundaries and blended into one concise, universal and indivisible entity. That is why nuances that were commonly associated with a certain instrument or a certain branch of music were also appropriately adapted and adroitly developed by the Ustad in order to fit them into the playing of other instruments and styles. To quote Shri Jotin Bhattacharya again, "He had suffered untold hardships and humiliations to combine the separate planning patterns into a common lore for all instruments."[7]

A creative musician who is a member of a certain *gharana* may and usually does further develop his style, originally obtained from his *guru*, by enriching and

6   "My Music, My Life" by Pandit Ravi Shankar.

7   "Ustad Allauddin Khan and His Music" by Jotin Bhattacharya.

expanding the same in the light of contributions by other masterminds in the field. What comprises his own contribution is the personal touch of originality and skill that he lends to it, resulting in a new, appealing and effective musical entity. But, if questioned about this, he may have to take recourse under the umbrella of the protective authority extended by his *gharana* (lineage/school). He can claim that there is a precedent for what he has done and trace it back to his own school's traditions. It is surprising that a musician like Ustad Allauddin Khan, who upheld the greatest traditions and brought into being many superb innovations can also be so uncharitably criticized even in the present days. Tansen, Sadarang and many other immortalized masters had the same problem to face early in their careers, but later on their innovations became part of our great musical heritage. In subsequent ages they became established as original innovators of classical music through the careers, activities and achievements of their disciples. Many such disciples, in their turns, had also added the spark of their own contributions and personality to their respective fields, not to the detriment of, or detraction from, their *gharanas* but for their further enrichment. Indian Classical Music has never stood in the same place, continuously achieving something new. It has been enriched by the new creative geniuses of successive generations.

Whenever Baba began performing a *raga*, the first thing he did was to concentrate his entire body and mind upon it. He, by his utmost devotion, went into its very soul. What blossomed out in course of this deep exercise was a compete *raga*, superbly plumed with all its glittering, multi-colored tenants and ornaments. What is more, the *raga*, thus developed and enriched further, became characterized by the artistic personality of the great maestro and became an original interpretation.

During a performance he would go down deep within himself. This process of absorption began right from the moment he concentrated his mind on the careful tuning of the *sarod* and its *tarafs* (sympathetic strings). When, in full control of his art yet with a kind of self-oblivious concentration, he cut himself off, by and by, from the outer world to set foot on the threshold of the *raga*, one could not help but be filled with feelings of reverence and wonder. To him, a *raga* was like a living person. He always proceeded slowly to create a living shape and substance for it. He was one of the rare ones who was able to connect so deeply that there would be an intimate union between music and the musician.

However, Baba was never satisfied with his achievements. He had said, "I have not finished, I have not still completed even my own training in music."

It will be interesting to mention here that Ustad Allauddin Khan had also composed several *bandishes* in *thumri* (semi-classical vocal form) which were also akin to *hori* (a type of classical song-form based on the legend of Radha and Krishna). These were *hori* compositions based on the characteristics of *thumri*, distinct from *hori-dhamar*. His *hori-thumri* compositions pertained to the *Benaras anga* (*anga* – form, or branch of expression). These he played from time to time. His aversion was not to *thumri* as such, but to that pattern of it, called *Punjabi anga*, which was in vogue in North-Western region of India. His liking for *hori* type of thumri stemmed from the fact that invariably its lyrical composition dealt with the divine love of Lord Krishna.

The old style of *thumri* represents a borderline between the more "serious" forms such as *dhrupad* and *khyal* and so-called "lighter" forms such as *geet, ghazal* and *bhajan*, oftentimes embodying a beautiful blending of these different varieties into one appealing and compact form. Baba also passed these on to his disciples as part of their training. He also liked to listen the singing of Siddheshwari Devi, a highly respected musician, whose *thumri* songs were composed and treated along the direction that he preferred in this specific area of the art.

Baba had a very high opinion of *dhrupad* (the oldest and most orthodox of the classical forms still in existence) and he knew many compositions of this very strict, yet profound, form of the art.

One day it so happened, when he had been in Paris touring with master dancer Uday Shankar's troupe, a number of women entered his room along with the famous dancer. Uday Shankar requested Baba to play some music for the curious ladies. Baba was not very enthusiastic about it, as he was sure that they would not be able to appreciate his music and so might not like it very much. But on their repeated requests, he relented and started playing on *sarod*, not with much heart in it. But soon he was surprised to notice that his desultory handling of the instrument did not go in vain with the unaccustomed small audience before him, who were listening to his music with tears in the eyes. Seeing them much moved by his playing, Baba started injecting into his music more and more life. When he stopped, there reigned in the room an atmosphere of perfect calm and bliss. Before taking leave, the women expressed their deep sense of gratitude to Ustad Allauddin Khan, saying that his music had removed all their strains and stresses, accumulated in their minds over the days and months, and healed them.

Baba did not allow his music to be commercialized and he was not focused on money. He dedicated his life to the cause of music and aspired after self-realization through the practice of music. Ustad Allauddin Khan's music bore vivid impressions of the real art.

In the early 20th century, Indian music was something least expected to be appreciated by Westerners. However, only one or two decades later, through the efforts of powerful Indian masters like Allauddin Khan and some others, the door to the understanding and appreciation of Indian music was eventually opened to Westerners for listening pleasure and even critical acclaim. At the time of Ustad Allauddin Khan's tour in Europe, from time to time, symposiums on Indian music and private sittings would be organized here and there. On one of these memorable occasions, the Ustad interpreted *Raga Bhimpalasri* before a very highly sophisticated audience. His excellent performance, marked by a very high order of melodic treatment and subtlety of nuances, created a formidable impression in the minds of the connoisseurs and artists gathered there. It was said that he drew tears from the eyes of many of the listeners. Partly due to Ustad Allauddin Khan's capable demonstrations, as aforementioned, Indian Music, both as a science and art, eventually secured its due place in Europe, and a great many Western art lovers and critics soon became able to follow and appreciate the treatment and development of the Indian *ragas*. Above all, Indian classical music, which even in India was given a wide berth by many as something dry and intellectual, became quite popular in Europe. European listeners who attended his performances were convinced that the scientific aspects of Indian music as well as its spiritual appeal were not moonshine, but tangible realities. The great welcome and appreciation that Ustad Allauddin Khan met with in Europe was a fulfillment of the prophecy of his *guru* Ustad Wazir Khan, that Allauddin's name would be immortalized through his achievements and contributions as a musician of the highest levels.

Baba was sometimes accused of having a rough attitude towards the *tabalchi* (tabla player). Although never disrespectful to the percussionists in any way, nor their noble art, he did not care for it if a *tabla* player, instead of cooperating with the main artist, vocal or instrumental, would try to outbid him or create complications for him by his convoluted ways of percussion playing. The *tabalchi's* accepted position is to attune himself to the style and diction of the main performer. Baba had to caution several tabla players of great repute and standing about their confused manner of doing things. He himself had garnered the most abstruse and minute knowledge of rhythm and naturally was eager to set the tabalchi on the right tract if the percussionist got derailed. His absolute command over *laya* (adherence to the prescribed speed and polyrhythmic mastery in strict tempo) made him an object of terror to many a *tabla* player.

Here it may be enlightening to quote Pandit Ravi Shankar on the point of Baba's handling of the percussionist, particularly tabla players. "The accompaniment of the *tabla* now has an extremely important role in Indian music, and instrumental music in particular. Even so, the status of the *tabla* accompanist until about thirty years ago was not especially high. Until recently, he was supposed to play only the *theka* (the basic sound syllables of a *tabla* combined to form phrases of rhythm as executed on drums) and the *sitar* or *sarod* player performed his fixed pieces or improvisations on the same rhythmic framework of a certain *taal*. Rarely did the *tabla* player have a chance to do more than a few very short pieces of solo improvisation during an entire performance. Even now, there are still some musicians who prefer the more passive accompaniment of the *tabla* player. It was primarily because my *guru* Allauddin Khan liked and encouraged the more active participation of the *tabla* accompanist, and because Ali Akbar Khan and I later promoted this, that the status of the *tabla* player as well as the proportion of *tabla* accompaniment in any piece have come to have so large a part in our music today."[8]

---

[8]   "My Music, My Life" by Pandit Ravi Shankar.

It is important to note here that it was Baba who helped the young and unknown *tabla* players to come into focus by giving them a chance to accompany him, a veteran and respected musician. This attitude indicates a unique large-heartedness in the world of Indian music in that era when masters used to feel a sort of degradation by singing or playing with a newcomer.

On one occasion in a concert, the renowned *sitarist* Ustad Enayat Khan and the celebrated *tabalchi* Ustad Azim Khan fell out with each other on some points or other in their performance together. The venue of this *mehfil* (musical gathering) was the Tripura Court. The matter at issue between them cropped up when on more than one occasion the two experts could not converge on *sam* (the first beat of the tala or rhythmic cycle being used). They started blaming each other for the mistakes. The Maharaja of Tripura intervened and suggested that Ustad Allauddin Khan be approached as a referee. Allauddin Khan gave his verdict in favor of Enayat Khan. His verdict at once became the final decree.

Another interesting anecdote might be cited here, testifying to the complete mastery that Baba had attained over even the most complex and subtlest of the rhythmic repertoire. A famous *ghatam* (tuned clay pot used as a percussion instrument) player from South India once visited the Maihar court. He was a master of all kinds of *tals* (rhythmic cycles) on the *ghatam*. He was asked to give percussion accompaniment to Baba in the very presence of His Highness, since he claimed that he would beat down Ustad Allauddin with his *ghatam* playing. At long last Baba selected an *ardha matra tal* (rhythmic cycle ending with a fraction of a beat instead of a whole one) with which the *ghatam* player could not cope, and so kept away from providing *ghatam* accompaniment to the master. However, he did not hesitate to give Baba his due place by owning up to the Ustad's supremacy in his command over rhythmic cycles and abstract work within a strict pulse.

An incident is cited here as an example of the effect Allauddin Khan's music was known to have.

It is said that one night Shankaran Namboodripad (Uday Shankar's *guru*), who had an image of Nataraj (the deity Shiva in the pose of Cosmic Dance) in his room, dreamed that Baba was going to play music for the gratification of Nataraj, the deity of the performing arts. On being told about it, Allauddin Khan became quite surprised, but only for a moment. He at once decided to bow to the divine will and play before the image of the deity. As such, he did fulfill the dream on his part. There one day, shortly after, he stood in front of Namboodri's apartment, sarod in hand – a picture as much of humility as of nobility. However, he did not go in directly, but stopped at the entrance. His hesitation was caused by his being a Muslim. In any case, he did not evade the attention of Namboodri, a member of the highest clan of proud Brahmins in Kerala. Choked with emotion, Namboodri took Baba inside, tears rolling down his cheeks. He made Allauddin sit in front of the Lord Nataraj's image so that the master musician may pour out his heart in streams of divine music. Shri Jotin Bhattacharya in his book, "*Ustad Allauddin Khan and His Music,*" has given a graphic description of the maestro and the environment he could create with his music: "Everyone was transported to the world of music, the abode of Nada Brahma. Baba was lost to himself as his fingers glided over ripples of divine notes with which the ancient rishis must have rung the banks of Mansarovar; notes that emerged from Mount Kailash and came wafted over the snows of the Himalayas and the laughter of the Alaknanda cascading down the Haridwar hillside and mingling with the soft notes of the sangam. When the nad-samadhi was over, Baba had to be awakened as if from anantashayanam, the deep primordial slumber in which he was lost. The reality was then a jarring and grating noise."[9]

On another occasion, Uday Shankar visited the All Bengal Music Conference in December 1934, which had attracted quite a large gathering of master musicians as well as lovers of the art. He had gone there with a special purpose. He sought a very expert Indian musician for his dance troupe, slated to tour Europe shortly thereafter. He would be very selective in choosing a master from the giants in this field who had assembled in the conference hall. For Shankar's purpose, an immaculate soloist who was also adept in orchestral composition and conducting, would be the most suitable. He instinctively set his mind upon Ustad Allauddin Khan, who answered all the requirements of the caliber of music director required for the famous dance group.

All through his life his whole being – his entire existence – had become attuned to music and the various musical instruments to which he had devoted himself. It was so much so that even in his last moments, when he was in a coma, persons around his deathbed noticed with tearful eyes how his palm and fingers were moving rhythmically, as if striking up *bols* on the tabla.

According to Allauddin Khan, *ragas* (the ancient melodic forms upon which all of Indian Classical Music is based) originated from God, and as such, he believed that success in music could only be achieved by His kind Grace.

Baba believed sincerely that his phenomenal success in various branches of music was made possible by divine inspiration and blessing. When we take account of his simple habits and detachment from the worldly luxuries and pleasures we cannot but wonder at the philosophy, mentality or motivation behind his way of life. It seems that Baba was fully conscious of the power of his music, as he felt confident in his heart that, not only to speak of human beings, his all-conquering notes could spread their magic even over birds and animals. To such a power, that which money and position can create is no match. Worldly possessions, therefore, held no charm for the inspired maestro. He was perfectly at peace with himself and wholly content that he enjoyed the love and regard of countless men, women and children his music had won over.

---

[9]   "Ustad Allauddin Khan and His Music" by Jotin Bhattacharya.

Whenever he elaborated on musical feelings and concepts, he seemed to be talking from the utmost depth of his heart, completely lost in the reverie of the exalted subject.

Baba's whole attitude in music was something more than, and beyond, the aesthetic. Of course, he fully sensed and appreciated the aesthetic beauty of his creations which even now are ranked among the most extraordinary musical compositions. About the span of his genius and his spiritual approach to music, Pandit Debu Chaudhuri has stated in one of his discourses on the maestro's art, "Ustad Allauddin Khan was not only a great musician but also a great composer. Besides being a musician and a composer, he was a great teacher. Such a combination can hardly be found in the history of Indian musicians. As a human being he was a dedicated soul – a soul which was dedicated to music and God. His strong belief in God made him a highly pious musician, which is once again a rare phenomenon, indeed."[10]

But it has been borne in mind, particularly by those who have not had the opportunity of coming in personal contact with him, that Allauddin Khan's aesthetic appreciation transcended the borders of sensuality. It was perfectly spiritual and meditative in its essence.

Let us consider the Ustad's own statement about the relationship between *taan* and *raga*. In his conception, "*Taan* does not always look eye to eye with *raga*, and the former is detrimental to the interest of the latter. *Taan* is worldly and associated with *tamasika* [profane] qualities and *raga* is heavenly, based on *sattvika* [pure or sublime] qualities. The former lacks the genius of expression, while the latter abounds in purity of expression."

Another feature of Baba's musical conceptualization was his complete belief in the purity and perfection of musical appeal. He was the last person to accept anything as belonging to the province of arts if it was impure or debauched. Indecency or even coarseness in musical taste or musical composition had no place whatsoever in his artistic view. In his perception, music as an art served to elevate our sensory faculties and consciousness to a much higher level.

Pandit Ravi Shankar spoke on the integrity of character and sense of moral and human values the great maestro always strove to help develop in his students. In the course of his appreciative remarks about his unique *guru*, Panditji stressed, "It was hard for anyone to abide by Baba's demands. His demands were great. He belonged to a very old school. That is why he was more or less like a *rishi* of our ancient 'ashram' period. At the time of training he wanted all his students to observe *brahmchaarya* [celibacy or continence], to have no luxurious life, starting from the clothes or doing of the hair or using scents. He was very much against all

---

[10]   Head of the Department of Music, Delhi University. The writer had a dialogue with Pandit Debu Chaudhuri in the course of which the above point was elicited.

these. He wanted that you must dress as much as necessary and not for fashion. He wanted that the whole way of life for his disciples should be like the way he went through in his own student life which is very difficult. It is very hard to lead life in this way in these days. But luckily in that period when I was at Maihar, it was so different. It was not like what it is today. At that time there were no cinema halls, now there are three or four cinema houses at Maihar so the whole thing is so different. Before there was no outside attraction or entertainment or anything else to take your mind away at Maihar. The whole atmosphere over there was charged with nothing else, but music and music only from morning to night, so that it was more difficult in a way than you find today."[11]

It must not be thought that Allauddin Khan wanted his music to convey only the rasas as simple sentiments of the human mind. He was very conscious and scrupulous about the intellectual perfection of artistic creativity. His juxtaposing and blending intellectualism with spirituality clashed little. His highly intellectual approach invariably transcended into sublime expressions of the spirit.

Baba was madly in love with his art every moment of the day and night. He adored music with the fervor of a selfless lover. His living moments had been completely filled with music whether in his conceptualization or in actual exercises. He wanted to nurture this impersonal, overwhelming love for music even after his ceasing to live in flesh and blood. Allauddin Khan often said that he should be buried in a place in his house where his pupils would be practicing music, for him to be in a position to hear their various notes even from inside his grave.

Baba's ideas about music closely resembled those of the world famous violinist Yehudi Menuhin, who says, "Yet, despite the strength of this spell, despite the domination of this one hypnotic mood, a characteristic of Indian music is that, far from deadening the intellect, it actually liberates the mind. This mathematical exercise becomes an ecstatic kind of astronomy which, without ever losing the physical impulse of momentary creation, carries the mind to a state where other considerations of body and reality become utterly remote."

Baba had profound knowledge in the theoretical areas of the musical art. He was well versed in the scientific aspects of music. He used to hear the discussions of these elements by various musicians during his training days at Rampur, and Allauddin Khan himself used to enlighten his students and patrons on the historical background of his *guru*, Ustad Wazir Khan, and his musical lineage, the *Senia gharana*.

THE SENIA GHARANA

During the Emperor Akbar's reign (ca 1550-1605 A.D.) there lived a musician named Sanmokhan Singh in a village in North India. He devoted himself to the

---

[11]   From writer's conversation with Pandit Ravi Shankar.

practice of his art whole-heartedly. He acquired such a high order of mastery over the *beena* that he was thought by many to have been groomed on it by no less a being than Lord Shiva (an aspect of the Hindu Trinity, who is also the Lord of Music) Himself. In a more mundane perspective however, his fine techniques were handed down through his family lineage.

Akbar was a connoisseur of merit and excellence in the arts and all areas of knowledge. He was always on the lookout for a worthy instrumental accompanist for his great court-musician Tansen, who was a vocalist of unparalleled excellence. When Akbar heard about Sanmokhan Singh, he planned to bring the master and make him his court-musician. One day Akbar, along with his ministers and Tansen, went to the temple in which Sanmokhan acted as a priest. As the handsome *Beenkar* came out of the temple with instrument in hand, Akbar expressed his desire for Sanmokhan to be a court-musician at Agra. But Singh refused the Emperor's proposal as he could not leave the temple, which he loved dearly. Mishir, Sanmokhan's son, was learning *beena* from his father and was already a musician of sorts. Akbar then requested Sanmokhan to allow Mishir to come with him to his court. Sanmokhan did not refuse Akbar this time. The emperor came back to his capital with the young boy.

Akbar became so much interested in Mishir's *beena* that he almost forgot Tansen, his legendary head musician. This pained the great vocalist. Tansen went to Swami Haridas, his *guru*, and took further training, this time in yet more advanced techniques and styles to score over Mishir. When Tansen returned, the two artists met in a musical sitting in presence of the emperor. It was Tansen's turn to outdo Mishir, and Mishir could not follow one of his *taans* which he had recently mastered from Swami Haridas. Desperate at his failure, Mishir threw a sword at Tansen to kill him, but luckily he was saved. Akbar became furious at his irresponsible conduct and ordered his advisor Birbal to take Mishir from his sight and behead him. But Birbal, being a man of legendary intelligence, took Mishir to his own house and hid him there.

Now it happened that after a long interval Akbar again felt inclined to hear Mishir's *beena* playing. Birbal pretended that Mishir had been dead. The emperor began to wail over Mishir's death and repented having ordered Birbal to execute him. Seeing his sincere sorrow and remorse, Birbal, desirous of disclosing the real truth about the whole affair, invited Akbar to his house to listen to his daughter play *beena*. The emperor was charmed by the playing which he thought was by Birbal's daughter. But he soon came to know that the instrument was played by Mishir, and not by Birbal's daughter. Thus Mishir was saved from the death sentence.

The emperor tried to find out some other way to make Mishir realize his guilt in trying to kill the vocal maestro Tansen. Akbar himself felt ashamed of having ordered the death penalty for Mishir. Eventually, Akbar found a solution. He asked the young musician to apologize to Tansen for his ill behavior, but Mishir was reluctant to do so because of Tansen being a "*Kshatriya*" (of the warrior caste, below the priestly caste of Mishir's father). Akbar then requested Tansen to forgive Mishir because of his tender age. Tansen agreed on one condition – that Mishir must marry his daughter Saraswati.

The emperor was happy with this proposal and the marriage took place with pomp and show. It was an important event in the history of music. With the marriage of Saraswati and Mishir, there was a union of two different styles and schools of music. In later years, Mishir became famous in the name of Nawbat Khan.

Ustad Wazir Khan was the proud descendant of Nawbat Khan. (This is the direct connection to the legendary Tansen, and thus the name *"Senia Gharana."*)

INTERPRETATIONS OF RAGAS

Baba provided comprehensive interpretations and commentaries on various *ragas*, besides affecting the further development of, and improvement upon, many others. Thanks to his missionary zeal, and the perseverance of some other rare geniuses in the field, this very subtle and fine creative art could be and can be maintained as a constantly flowing stream, instead of it being lost in the sands of time and obsolescence.

Let us take his treatment of *Raga Sarang*.

A peculiarity of *Sarang* is that it uses double Ni (7ths) and excludes Ga (3rd), but in Baba's creative conception it was incomplete to some extent, limiting the entire beauty of *Sarang*. So he insisted on using *ishat* or "light" Ga in its interpretation. It should be noted that Tansen himself and, following him, the *Senia Gharana* as a whole used and would use Ga as an indispensable component of the *Sarang* structure. To prove his point, Baba vividly showed how the use of Ga made *Sarang* a more interesting and appealing raga through many a practical demonstration.

Baba developed and interpreted *Raga Bilaval* in the style of the great pioneering virtuoso Tansen. Tansen's *Bilaval*, although freely drawing upon the several types of it prevalent in the country, crystallized into a unique and most beautiful form. At Baba's able hands and through his creative genius, Tansen's *Bilaval* was further enriched and became one of the sweetest melodic forms in Indian musicology. It is interesting to quote the famous pakhawaj master Ayodhya Prasad in this connection. He had said, "I was lucky to hear *Alhayia-Bilaval* (a derivative-raga of *Bilaval*) from Ustad Allauddin Khan for which I have no (adequate) words of praise. It was simply marvelous."

The writer's father was privileged to hear many talks given by Allauddin Khan, included in which were legendary stories of the *Senia* line, in particular the almost mythological accounts of the great Tansen's musical feats. Once, Baba recounted the story of two other famous musicians of Tansen's time – Suraj Khan and Chand Khan. These two brothers lived at Tilmandi, a village in Punjab. Suraj Khan had great expertise in all *ragas* which usually were thought fit to be played between sunrise and sunset. Chand Khan, on the other hand, possessed absolute command over the *ragas* generally played between sunset and sunrise – the exact opposite of his great brother Suraj Khan.

The two, one after another, kept on playing music throughout the 24 hours of the day and night – Suraj Khan from dawn to dusk and Chand Khan from dusk to dawn. It so happened that they became eager to roam about India and win fame as artists far superior to any other. In course of their travels they arrived at the Mughal court at the beautiful capital city of Fatehpur Sikri. There they challenged Tansen himself.

In the competition that followed, Suraj Khan and Chand Khan sang all of the "primary" ragas (precisely – six "male" ragas and the 36 "female" *ragas* (*raginis*) associated with them) within the span of 24 hours in a single session. Now it was Tansen's turn to establish his supremacy. But how? The two Khans had covered all of the primary *ragas* with nothing left for Tansen to sing but recapitulate some already handled by them. However, Tansen was not the type of man to be deterred so easily. He at once conceived altogether new and original *ragas* and sang superbly for 24 hours straight. Tansen continued singing the freshly invented *ragas*, one after another – from *Kaushi Bhairav* to *Dhanasri* – spanning the entire period of 24 hours of the day and night. At the end, Suraj Khan and Chand Khan, who appreciated his superiority over them, became his disciples. Several of the new creations of Mian Tansen were named respectively as *Kaushi-Bhairav, Kaushi-Bhairavi, Mian Ki Todi, Lakshmi Todi, Darbari Todi, Shudha-Bilaval, Yamni-Bilabal, Mian Ki Sarang, Suha Sughrai, Barari, Dhanasri, Puria-Dhanasri* and the like.

After the manner of Tansen, the great sarod-player Ustad Allauddin Khan, in our times, could also play a *raga* for hours on end without any sign of boredom or fatigue whenever he had an occasion to play before an audience that could appreciate his high art. And when he played songs meant for vocal rendering on an instrument, he was known to create the melodic atmosphere as would be created by a great vocalist of skill and sonority.

Shri S. N. Ratanjankar, the legendary scholar, singer of the *Agra Gharana* and principal of Bhatkhande Sangeet Vidyapeeth in Lucknow said, "It is no wonder that today Ustad Allauddin Khan is the acknowledged leader among the instrumental musicians of North India."

At home and abroad in Europe, Baba won many awards and laurels of triumph and appreciation, and critically acclaimed reviews of his performances were featured in scores of newspapers. The writers often compared him with the great masters of the past, both of Indian Classical Music and the legends of European Classical Music.

In his interview with the Maharaja of Maihar in connection with the post of royal musical teacher, Ustad Allauddin Khan was asked to demonstrate his proficiency in any *raga* of his liking. Baba began playing the very difficult, although profound, *Raga Shri*. He gradually developed the theme of the *raga*, incrementally increasing momentum and tempo. Upon reaching a climactic point in the thrilling atmosphere created by Baba's rendition of the *raga*, the Maihar Maharaja could stand the intensity of feeling no longer. The performance had proved to be beyond the Maharaja's threshold of being enthralled for such an uninterrupted period. He abruptly got up and bent down to the master, saying, "Oh! Ustad, please stop at once! I cannot bear the intoxicating and sublime charm that you have created with your expert treatment of the *raga!*"

AS A RENOVATOR OF SAROD

Baba was not satisfied with the limitations caused by the structure of the *sarod.* The type of music he wanted to create on the instrument needed an improved version of it. This was quite understandable. He was never content with the stereotyped or, for that matter, with the existing bounds and peripheries of any *raga*, far be it an instrument. He was after great and still greater achievements. To him the point of perfection in any branch of music or instrument was not fixed but ever-expanding. He sought ever growing and dynamic development of every *raga*, and even of the instruments as the vehicles.

He found the *sarod* as it was at that time as not wholly suitable for bringing out all the nuances of *ragas* properly and that its sonority needed further improvement. Therefore, he thought it fit to introduce a few innovations to the structure and mechanism of sarod. Originally it had only five main strings plus two *chikaris* (drone strings), tuned Sa and Sa, and not more than nine strings for the *tarafs* (resonating or sympathetic strings). Baba introduced an improved version of *sarod* with a greater number of operative *baz* (playing) strings and 16 *tarafs*. Although formerly five *baz* strings were considered ideal, but in actual practice, only four of these were used. Baba emphasized using all five *baz* strings. His renovations went a long way towards improving the tonal aspects of the sarod. He also altered the size and structure of the instrument in order to facilitate easy handling and help somewhat the aesthetic beauty of its appearance.

CHANDRASARANG

Ustad Allauddin Khan's creativity went to the extent of inventing an altogether new instrument, which he named *Chandrasarang*. In the countryside of Bengal a very popular instrument is the *sarinda*, which resembles the *sarangi* in size and appearance and needs, like the latter, a bow to produce the tones. Baba's *Chandrasarang* was a mixture of the Western violin and the *sarinda*. Some of his students learned how to play on the new instrument which, however, has not yet become common and popular like *sarod*, *sitar*, and *violin*, etc.

INTRODUCTION OF NEW RAGAS

Baba also made valuable contributions to the field of musicology in several ways. We have already discussed how he affected a much needed and welcome synthesis of the distinct and separate styles of different instruments. We have also touched upon his synthesizing approach to both vocal and instrumental music. He adorned and enriched the art in another way as well. With his acute insight into the melodic and dramatic conceptualizations of all the *ragas* in vogue, he, very spontaneously and in the usual course of things, conceived many sets of tonal arrangements, with the result that in every *raga* he could improvise endlessly. However, his creative genius could not rest content with the existing sets of *ragas*. He needed more *ragas* as vehicles for his musical ideas. He unveiled several new *ragas*, such as *Madan Manjari, Bhuvaneshwari, Manjh-Khamaj, Bhagawati, Muhammad, Subhavati, Dhavaleswari, Kedar-Manjh, Hemant*, and several others.

On the actual technique of playing sarod, he developed new approaches for the right and left hands for greater range of expression in any tempo. These new techniques spread to many other musicians who made profuse use of them. Almost all of his original innovations eventually became standard.

BABA'S MICRO TIMINGS (TALAS WITH FRACTIONAL BEATS)

Baba's control over timing or *laya* in music was total. Whether instrumentally or vocally, every composition or piece in Indian Classical Music is played within with some particular time cycle, within which the compositions and improvisations – or extemporizations – of the *raga* being used. Baba's unique contribution in the sphere of *laya* (tempo, timing and polyrhythms in Indian music) also consisted of introducing several new time cycles or *talas* which ended in ardha-matra or half-beat. (It must be noted that fractional *talas* were used in Indian Music previously, but Allauddin Khan introduced particular types.) However, these fractional cycles were not used much in his public compositions or performances. To satisfy one's curiosity, several of these *ardha-matrik talas* are being noted below –

(i)	Mohantal	3 1/2 matras
(ii)	Rajbeshtal	4 1/2 matras
(iii)	Udavsintal	5 1/2 matras
(iv)	Upatal/Upatal Jhampak	8 1/2 matras
(v)	Bikramat tal	9 1/2 matras
(vi)	Laghukirtital	10 1/2 matras
(vii)	Bangaravattal	13 1/2 matras
(viii)	Abhinandatal	14 1/2 matras
	etc., etc.	

Some traditional talas which were and are very seldom utilized also came to life under his conception and treatment. These were as follows:

(i)	Mattatal	9	matras
(ii)	Kokitatal	1	matra
(iii)	Jagmohantal	11	matras
(iv)	Shankartal	11	matras
(v)	Panchamsawarital	15	matras
(vi)	Laxmital	18	matras

CONCEPT AND APPLICATION OF TEMPO WORK

Regardless of the aritst's command over the tonal side of music, without an appropriate command of tempo – and without understanding the proper acceleration of such, as particularly necessary for Indian Classical Music – even the best possible composition may not be played as effectively and attractively. Baba's approach, besides answering the requirements of the tonal interpretation of a *raga*, attached great importance to the tempo factor.

After creating the atmosphere and temperament, set up by an inspired and improvised *alapchari* (alap), Baba would begin a *gat* (composition that is set up for improvisation in a rhythmic cycle, accompanied by percussion) in *Masitkhani vilambit* (a particular type of slow and extended compositional framework). Then he almost imperceptibly glided into the realm of *vistar* (expansion of the *raga* within *tala*, using the composition only as a place to rest), gradually to accelerate the pace, putting forward *bols* (syllabic patterns) and *taans* (musical lines) while still working in a slow tempo, although a little quicker than before. This tempo could be called *madhya vilambit* (medium-slow) *gat*. Then, for the purpose of giving shape, *alankars* or *paltas* and ornamentations with *gamaks, tans, meends, murchhanas*, etc., were used. He now hastened his pace a bit more, making the *sthai* (main segment of the composed part) keep to a *madhya* (medium) *gat* pattern. In successive stages, *layakari* (polyrhythmic work) and the final section of the *Masitkani* were played in a still further accelerated tempo. At this stage it turned into a *madhya drut* (medium fast) *gat*, or alternatively *Rezakhani gat*, in which he was an accomplished master as well.

For some time he would go on with his interpretation of the raga, now further enriched with sundry kinds of *alankars* (permutations) in *drut* (fast) *gat* (*Rezakhani*), maintaining the foundation *laya* (tempo) in the original *sthai*. He would then quicken the tempo and climb into what is called *ati drut* (very fast) *gat*, culminating in a climax. The befitting finale was expressed through the use of high-speed *jhala* and *dhuamatha* (rhythmic musical devices using the resonance of the instrument).

What transpired at the end of the performance was a experience of thrilling sensation and ecstasy saturating the minds of the audience.

THE MAIHAR BAND

Ustad Enayat Khan, the legendary sitarist and retained musician of the Gauripur Estate (now in Bangladesh) and a contemporary of Baba, once recorded his high evaluation of the Maihar Band founded by Ustad Allauddin Khan thus: "Allauddin Khan is a famous sarod player and a man of knowledge. I do not know what other instruments he plays but his Maihar Band is a superb thing. He is the founder and composer of this Band."

The Maihar Band was a unique institution reflecting great credit upon Ustad Allauddin Khan's musical genius, organizational expertise and last, but not least, his deep humanist feelings. There were many orchestral groups that he brought into being and led. His orchestral compositions were as original and masterful as they were varied. One of these groups was his Maihar State Band, which was distinguished by the human elements involved in it. The musicians of the Band, numbering no fewer than 150, were mostly youngsters between the ages of eight and 16. How he gathered these boys of the Band is another magnificent story of his deep sympathy for the distressed.

He could not but pick up a child as his own whenever he came to know that it was forlorn and uncared for. He brought home a great many of these destitute children and fed them. His duty did not end there. He was not a man to be content without sharing with them his artistic joys. Not only did he train them in music, he also set up an orchestra with them. It became the famous Maihar State Band, which earned laurels by playing at the fourth All-India Music Conference, held at Lucknow in 1925, on 9th and 11th January. Besides Ustad Allauddin, the band's director and conductor, it had 17 budding musicians who gave excellent performances in the *Ragas Yaman-Kalyan*, *Tilak-Kamod*, and *Khamaj*.

Then they performed Indian marching-band compositions as part of the program. The Band had three *sitars*, two *violins*, two *dilrubas*, two *flutes*, two *tablas*, one *sarangi*, one *triangle*, one *viola* and one *naltaranga*, a type of metallophone. Because of their high level of playing, the tender-aged artists received warm appreciation and the Maihar Band was presented with a gold medal. The Maihar State Band was not a fluke affair. Subsequently over the years, during Baba's lifetime the Maihar State Band continued to be a very active institution, adding cultural richness to the life of the people in the state and many other places.

ORGANIZATIONAL ABILITY

Baba was always engrossed in the intoxication of music. Even when he was not playing on an instrument or singing, he was deeply absorbed in meditating upon the various aspects of the art. As already stated in the preceding chapters, Allauddin Khan's temperament was philosophical. His thoughtful and contemplative disposition was natural. Therefore, it is amazing to consider how he could formulate and execute schemes to build up institutions which needed practical plans and management abilities. He was not only pragmatic, but possessed great organizational capacity. The best monument to his organizational skill was the Maihar Music College. He was not only the guiding spirit of this great institution, but controlled and managed its day-to-day activities in a very efficient manner. He was the founder and the first principal of this celebrated institution for giving providing training in music.

WAZIRKHANI GAT

Baba named certain *gats* as "Wazirkhani," named after his revered *guru*, whose *bols* were not similar to those of *Masitkhani gats*, as exemplified below –

Masitkhani gat:

diri da diri da ra da da ra,
diri da diri da ra da da ra

Although *Wazirkhani gats* were few, the *bols* of such *gats* are given below:

da diri da ra da diri da ra
da da ra diri da diri da
diri da ra da ra da ra

ALLAUDDIN GHARANA

Ustad Allauddin Khan's oceanic knowledge of music and the deep impress of his originality upon various trends and aspects of musical composition, peculiar to his *guru's gharana* (*Senia*) or, for the matter of that any other school or *gharana*, led and even now lead critics and connoisseurs to brand his productions into an altogether separate and specific school or *gharana*. And they would like to call it his own *gharana*. i.e., Allauddin *Gharana*. Of course, there are others who do not want to go to the extent of ascribing a new *gharana* to him. However, the second group of music lovers and critics do not hesitate to give him credit for his remarkable genius and his great many original innovations in the area of North Indian Classical Music.

SITARKHANI-THEKA (Sitarkhani tabla pattern)

Ustad Allauddin Khan often played *gats* which were his original creations. Some of these *gats* were accompanied on the *tabla* in *addha theka* or *sitar-khani theka* of 16 beats, which substituted for the primarily used Tritaal or Tinaal (also of

16 beats)(*Theka: the exact syllables that make up a tala and its feel.*) An example such a *bandish* (composition) used by the Ustad is noted below:

Raga: Jhinjhoti Tala: Sitarkhani (16 beats) Time: Evening

Sthai

```
N Ḍ - N | P Ḍ S R | G R - M | G - - -
| | - o | | o | o | | | - o | | - - -
0         3         x         2
```

```
N Ḍ - N | P Ḍ S R | G R - M | G S - Ḍ
| | - o | | | | o | | | - o | | | - o
0         3         x         2
```

```
N - - R | N Ḍ P Ḍ | M PP M P | Ḍ S R G
| - - | | | o | o | | v | o | | o | o
0         3         x         2
```

```
S RR M P | D Ṡ - N | D P - M | G - - -
| v | o | | o - o | | | - o | | - - -
0         3         x         2
```

Antara

S RR MP	D Ṡ -Ṡ Ṡ	Ṡ ṚṚ ĠĠ ṚṚ	Ṡ ṢṆ -N D
I v Io	Io - Io	I v v v	I oI - Io
0	3	x	2

ṢṠ ṢṠ N ND	-D P PP DD	M MG -G M
v v I oI	-o I v v	I oI -o I
0	3	x

G GS -S R
I   oI -o I
2

Baba used to say that one should feel like dancing when one heard or played one's instrument in the above *theka*. He was fond of making the Sa (tonic) his *sam* (beat number 1). There are many gats in which he had showed this inclination.

Baba created his compositions at any time in the course of the day. Even as he went on with his household chores, his mind roamed about in the realm of music, resulting in the conception and formulation of many a *gat* (composition). A specimen is given below:

Raga: Bhairavi* Tala: Tritaal in Madhya Laya (medium tempo) Time: Morning

S DD P D	- P M P	G - S R	G G M -
I v Io	- I I o	I - I o	I o I -
0	3	x	2

- S G R	S SD -D P	P DD P D	N S R S
- I o I	I oI -o I	I v I o	I o I o
0	3	x	2

S R GG MM	G GR - R S	D - P -	M G R S
l o v v	l ol -o l	l - o -	l o l o
0	3	x	2

[*Although Baba was fond of Raga Bhairavi, he was not inclined to play it out of sorrow after the death of his daughter Jananara, who used to dance to this Raga, wearing rings on her hand.]

As has been mentioned before, Baba was also a lyricist of sorts. He composed lyrics mainly in Bengali, quite a few having been couched in Hindi as well. All these lyrics were set to appropriate tunes by himself.

HONORS

For his extraordinary achievements in the field of music, Ustad Allauddin Khan received many awards, titles and prizes, and also held distinguished positions.

Baba first came to Maihar as the court-maestro and musical *guru* of the state's ruler, the Maharaja.

As already stated previously, Allauddin Khan participated in the fourth All India Music Conference, held in Lucknow in 1925 at Kaisarbagh, Baradari (the former palace of the last king of Oudh, Nawab Wazid Ali Shah, a great musician and a patron of music). Besides being hailed as a versatile master of outstanding abilities, he also gained no fewer than four gold medals at the conference. These medals were given respectively by Raja Sahib Shivgarh, Raja Moti Chand of Varanasi, Shri Dilip Kumar Roy, and Gurindra Pandit Satu. These dignitaries were respected as either connoisseurs or masters of Indian Classical Music. Baba, for his tremendous renditions of *Ragas Kafi* and *Tilak-Kamod*, was also given a financial award in addition to the concert fee anonymously.

His performances on all three days of the session were not only evaluated as workmanship of the highest quality by a distinguished board of judges – all of them were giants in the field – but also charmed the general audience. The board of judges consisted of the following personages of eminence :

(i)   Pandit Vishnu Narayan Bhatkhande, Bombay
(ii) Thakur Mohammad Nawab Ali Khan, Lucknow
(iii) Shri Shivendra Nath Basu Sahib, Varanasi
(iv) Professor Prem Vallabh Joshi, Ajmere
(v)   Shri Dilip Kumar Roy, Calcutta.

The Lucknow music conference became a landmark in the history of Indian music for another great achievement. The excellent standard of the various branches of Indian music, displayed in several sittings of the conference by eminent artists like Ustad Allauddin Khan and others of the same caliber, created such deep enthusiasm all around that it was decided that a concrete shape be given to satisfy the hearts of artists and lovers of music by founding a worthy and well-equipped institution for the dissemination of musical education and training in the most elaborate and comprehensive manner. As a result, the Morris College of Hindusthani Music, renamed now as Bhatkhande Sangeet Vidyapeeth, came into being. The music college was named after Sir William Sinclair Morris, the then Governor of the United Provinces (now Uttar Pradesh), to make the provincial government interested in the new scheme. For many years, Baba was associated with the Morris College as an examiner.

The Lucknow Music Conference did not fail to express its appreciation of Ustad Allauddin Khan's work as an educator of music and builder of artists. For meritorious performance, the Maihar Band was highly assessed at the conference. A medal was awarded by Raja Sahib Tiwara and a financial award in cash was given for its superb performance. One of Baba's students, Jhurra, was awarded a special gold medal by Pandit Gokaran Nath Misra. This young artist, a find by Allauddin Khan himself, played on *Jaltaranga* (musical water bowls) in the Band.

When the Maihar Music College was established, he became its first principal, a post he held until his death. Baba's reputation did not remain confined to the boundaries of the state of Maihar alone. It spread not only all over India but also beyond the country's frontiers to the world at large, particularly in Europe.

During the All-India Industrial and Agricultural exhibition held in Lucknow in 1936, a music conference was also arranged as a distinctive feature of the function. Baba was one of its foremost participants. As was usual, wherever he went, laurels came his way. His stamp of excellence was displayed at the conference and was universally recognized. Allauddin Khan's already exalted reputation as one of the most talented and many-sided musicians, was now shining brighter than ever.

Upon hearing the sitar of Pandit Ravi Shankar, Maharaj Kumar of Jodhpur was very eager to hear the sarod of Ustad Allauddin Khan (Shankar's teacher). In June of 1945, Maharaj Kumar sent an invitation to Ustad Allauddin through his court-musician, Shri Annada Adhikari, an invitation Baba accepted. Baba came to Jodhpur palace and stayed for 11 days instead of the committed 3 or 4 days. During his stay, he gave several demonstrations of his art in the presence of the Maharaj Kumar himself. His performances pleased the prince very much and Allauddin Khan was amply rewarded by the Maharaj Kumar. From the next year onward, Ali Akbar Khan (Allauddin Khan's illustrious sarod-playing son) was appointed as the court-musician of Jodhpur State. Maharaj Kumar had a great regard for Baba.

In 1950, Baba was appointed as Head of Department in the department of instrumental music in Benares Hindu University, which he did not accept at the end. Ustad Allauddin Khan was also made a *"Fellow of Sangeet Natak Akademi"* (National Academy of Performing Arts). He was invested in 1958 by the Vishwa Bharati, founded by the immortal world-poet Rabindranath Tagore at Shantiniketan, with the degree of *"Doctor of Music"* (*honoris causa*).

In 1958, the Government of India placed on record its recognition and appreciation of the unique achievements of Ustad Allauddin Khan as a grand master by presenting him with the title of *"Padmabhushan."* He was one of the first four to receive this covetous national award.

As far as his music was concerned, Allauddin Khan played it wholeheartedly and untiringly almost until the last years of his life. He never grew old in spirit or senile in mind. In this field he remained ageless. On the occasion of the Aurobindo birth anniversary in 1959 at Park Circus in Calcutta before a packed and appreciative audience, Allauddin Khan's grandson Ashish Khan played with him on sarod. It was a historic performance of the grandfather and the grandson duo. It was said that Baba did not evince the least stress of fatigue in course of the entire duration of his gripping performance. He was then 91 years old.

Further adding to his glory was the Vishwa Bharati giving him the title of *"Deshi-ko-Uttam"* in 1954. And in 1971, Ustad Allauddin Khan was honored by the Government of India with the title of *"Padma Vibhushan"* (the second highest State awarded title possible). Baba was also invited to be the state musician of the State of Baroda with a high salary, but he rejected that offer because of his affection for, and a sense of loyalty to, the Maharaja of Maihar, under whom he had been serving for many years as his *guru*. Baba was bestowed the highest rank, next only to Sardar and Minister, by the Maharaja of Maihar. He also received the title of *Aftab-e-Hind* from Tansen Sangeet Samiti, *Sangeetacharya* from Bhatkhande Sangeet Vidyapeeth, *Sangeet Nayak* by the Nawab of Rampur and also earned the national designation of *"Bharat-Gaurav"* (the "Pride of India"). Ustad Allauddin Khan was honored with the degree of *"Doctor of Music"* in absentia by the Indira Kala Sangeet Vishwa Vidyalaya of Khairagarh.

In recognition of the great master's genius and achievements in music and to pay tribute to him, the Government of Madhya Pradesh (in which the former Vindhya Pradesh is included) began a new institution after Baba's passing. For the upliftment of artists, the Madhya Pradesh Kala Parishad has been renamed after the great pioneer as Ustad Allauddin Khan Academy. It organizes various cultural activities such as "Arambha" for the young and rising musicians at the end of every three months of its session. Besides, "Utsav" (large function), a seminar on *Kathak* (the highest dance form of North Indian Classical dance), a festival of dances at Khajuraho, an exhibition of rare instruments, etc., are also some of the features the Ustad Allauddin Khan Academy undertakes every year for enlightening art lovers and laymen alike on the great musician's achievements, and to motivate and encourage artists. It also goes to the credit of the academy that it spares no pains to highlight the various worthy tenets of several other *gharanas* (schools) of Indian music and expound upon the basic aspects of this refined and subtle aesthetic subject from a general perspective.

The Bharat Ram Foundation also began a music conference under his name: "Baba Allauddin Sangeet Samaroh."[12]

One after another, various persons – connoisseurs and musicians both – who had an opportunity to be closely associated with the maestro during his lifetime are coming forth with valuable tracts and documentaries, focusing attention on his extraordinary genius and outstanding achievements in the different fields of the art. Amongst these, Pandit Ravi Shankar's documentary film on Ustad Allauddin Khan illuminates several aspects of the master's art.

When mentioning other writers' works on Allauddin Khan, one must credit Rajendra Shankar, Jotin Bhattacharya, Mubarak Hussain Khan (his nephew and his youngest brother Ayat Ali Khan's son), and others. Their works have been duly noted in the bibliography of this book.

It was just like Baba that all his honors – official and non-official did not make even a little difference to his way of life. He remained the same simple and gentle man till the end. Pandit Ravi Shankar has said, "Thus, honor and recognition came to him in the evening of his life, but he remains, following the saying in the Geeta, unmoved and unruffled as he pursues his work and the study of music, never bothering, never worrying or looking back."[13]

---

[12] Writer knows it from Shri Rebati Ranjan Debnath.

[13] "My Music, My Life" by Pandit Ravi Shankar.

Chapter 6

THE MASTER'S RECORDINGS

THOUGH USTAD ALLAUDDIN Khan recorded his music infrequently, some of his best compositions are found there. It is entirely possible that he considered the limited span of a record unsuitable for his music which was characterized by elaborate and creative improvisation, filling not only a few minutes but oftentimes hours. However, on repeated requests from his admirers and record company executives, he had to relent sometimes and consent to record his music, making the best of the very limited time available on the old 78 RPM discs. Unfortunately, the very few records that he made are not readily available in tact because of neglect. Some of his records were ruined, and only those few which could evade the ravages of time or the usual wear and tear have been preserved at the National Archives in India. So these are not readily available to the public. Under the circumstances, detailed reviews of these records are not possible. Naturally our attention would remain confined to the assessment and appreciation of about only half a dozen records. *Sarod*, violin, *surbahar* and *rabab* formed the medium of his music in these discs. Three or four recordings are in the name of the Maihar State String Band.

A list of his records is given below:

1. *Sarod*   Megaphone JNG 924

(The *raga* in question could not be ascertained as no disc of this recording is available.)

2. *Sarod*		Megaphone JNG 192

Side one – *Jila Vilambit*
Side two – *Lalit*

3. *Sarod*	–	Megaphone JNG 6020

Side one – *Bihag*
Side two – *Tilak–Kamod*

Megaphone Record, Long Play 33 1/3 RPM

4. *Sarod* – *Lalit*
Jila Vilambit
Tilak-Kamod
Bihag
Bhairavi
Gara

5. *Violin* – *Sindhura*
Bihag
Maru-Khamaj
Malgunja
Kirtan

It would have been beneficial for artists and art critics as well as for orchestra players, if the recorded discs with the marks of G.C. B 10177, 10178 and G.C. P 6563 (recordings by The Gramophone Company of India), played by the Maihar State Band, had been recovered from their regrettable fate.

The recordings of the Maihar State Band were:

Majuma Sanja	–	*Sitarkhani, Khamaj, Ektal*
Majuma Sanja	–	*Tilak-Kamod, Tha-Dun, Chautal*
Majuma Sanja	–	*Hindusthani Posta Dadra*
Majuma Sanja	–	*Hindusthani Posta Ektal*

Chapter 7

BABA'S DISCIPLES

USTAD ALLAUDDIN KHAN was one of the greatest teachers of Indian Music in its history, as demonstrated by the unusually large number of eminent musicians who had learned from him as their principal guru. The front ranks of such luminary artists trained by him are occupied not only by his son, daughter, son-in-law, grandsons and other family relations, as well as many other well-known talents outside the family.

Allauddin Khansaheb, having been himself a dedicated and devoted person, always insisted on all his students to have unadulterated sincerity of purpose and deep devotion in their musical ambitions. To mold them into his ideal of a perfect artist, he would leave no stone unturned. He would see to it that they would put in copious numbers of hours of the most attentive and indefatigable labor. Amateurish lightheartedness or nonchalance, in his perspective, was anathema to a sincere student of music. Therefore, he would see that all his students regularly practice and master the lessons set by him, systematically and with pious devotion. His presence and activity at Maihar, otherwise a small, out-of-the-way town, made it a famous art center, aspirants of music flocking to it from all the corners of the country, and sometimes even from foreign lands. Although he is no more, his great heritage is undying and is being carried on by several masters of outstanding abilities, which the late genius himself helped develop.

Allauddin Khan's disciples were many and quite a few of them set their own mark of distinction and glory. First and foremost was his patron and employer, His Highness, the Maharaja of Maihar, who took lessons from the Ustad in various branches of vocal music. Among his *sarod* students, in the forefront were Ustad Ali Akbar Khan (son), Timir Baran, Bahadur Khan (nephew), Projesh Banerjee, Sharan Rani (Backliwal), Suprabhat Pal and others. The late Pannalal Ghosh was among the most outstanding students who received training in flute. His disciples of distinction on sitar were Pandit Ravi Shankar, Rani Mitter (he was a sitarist at "Prithvi Raj Theater" afterwards), Pandit Nikhil Banerjee, Mrs. Sheela Bharat Ram, Rebati Ranjan Debnath, Sripada Bandopadhyaya, Idri Singh, Sachin Dutta, Protima Roy Chowdhury, Arun Bharat Ram, Mrs. Swarnalata Chopra among several others. Phatik Saha (a radio artist in Dhaka), Naidu and Jotindranath Banerjee were among his foremost violin students. Baba's *esraj* students were Anil Dev Burman and Chitta Dev Burman, Ghurrey Maharaj, Binay Bharat Ram (among others) and his *harmonium* students of repute were Ram Pyaro and Gulgul Maharaj.

Baba also trained his youngest brother, Ayat Ali Khan, who revolutionized *surbahar* playing by introducing to it western style compositions. Ustad Ayat Ali Khan afterwards adorned the Maihar and Rampur *durbar* as a court musician.

Many amongst other celebrated artists also traced their skill in their respective fields to the training they received at the hands of the venerable maestro. Some of them are: *sitar* group – Dyuti Kishore Acharya, Shubhendra Shankar, Balai Banerjee, Indraneel Bhattacharya, Bibek Ranjan Singha, Hiren Mukherjee, Khalem Hussain (Baba's younger brother Nayab Ali's son), Nirmal Kumar Roy Chowdhury, etc. *sarod* group – Ashish Khan, Dhyanesh Khan (both grandsons), Vasant Rai, C.L. Das, Sanat Banerjee, etc.; violin group – Robin Ghosh, etc.; *Chandrasarang* group – Jiten Golui, Ranjit Banerjee, etc.

Besides these, many non-Indians also learned the art under his personal instruction and care. Of these, mention may be made of Srimati Indira Debi.

Baba had the distinction of coaching countless budding artists many amongst whom in the course of years had established themselves as top level musicians both within and outside the country. His students hailed from a cross-section of the social matrix – Some being well-to-do and others quite poor. Before his undiscriminating eyes they were all equal, without any distinction of religion, caste or social status. In his perspective, the overwhelmingly important factor was their burning zeal for music. He never discouraged anyone. Success depended on earnestness and perseverance with Baba's meticulously designed musical lessons and courses.

Even those aspirants who were not his students or who might have actually had other teachers or *gurus* also found him ever obliging whenever they had any occasion to approach him for imparting training to them, especially in regard to those peculiar features of his own invention or some difficult notes or *laya* they could not tackle properly. Many from outside his own group of students would approach him for instruction.

He was terribly shaken when his disciples, the Maharaja of Maihar and Pannalal Ghosh passed away. To him this was not mere sorrow at the demise of two able disciples, but real severe bereavements and losses that perhaps only a son or daughter's death might cause. His paternal feelings for the good of his disciples can be judged from the fact that he invariably remonstrated anyone who wanted to spend money on Baba and insisted that he/she had better spend it for his/her own children or others in the family at home.[14]

Allauddin Khan was eager only for his students' own welfare – their own progress in the training in the art. He earnestly wished for their highest accomplishment and greatest success.

It was a regular ambition and even a lifelong preoccupation with Baba to find meritorious pupils. As he himself withstood indescribable hardships and trials as a pupil, not only for one or two years, but for several years at a stretch without succumbing, he looked for pupils of the sort he himself had been. He was often heard to comment: "*Guru mile lakhe-lakhe, chela mile na ek.*" (Meaning: there may be thousands of teachers, but not even one real student.)

He was aware that serious and sincere pupils of music are not easily found. Sincerity of purpose and devotion to one's idea is not common, so whenever he chanced to have a student, exclusively and seriously given to the training of music as the be-all and end-all of his life, he considered himself greatly fortunate.

Baba advised his pupils to practice hard and attain so much that anyone would know them as musicians of high caliber the moment he or she chanced to listen to their performance. Arduous practice would give them mastery over their subject to such an extent that simply a small patch of their music would give ample evidence of their unique skill, without the need for a prolonged or elaborate performance. He would say that a skilled cook could immediately find out whether the whole pot of rice was fully cooked or not by examining only one grain. Likewise, by listening to a small piece played by a master, his entire merit and worth could be ascertained.

Now it would be edifying to throw light upon some of his senior disciples. Several of them in later years succeeded in developing Baba's musical style and innovation still further and impressed them with the stamp of their own acumen and unique character.

USTAD ALI AKBAR KHAN

Baba started teaching music to his only son Ali Akbar Khan from the age of three. He taught him in his usual fashion, but was particularly strict and exacting with his very talented son. When Ali Akbar reached the age of five he was initiated on the *sarod* by his father. Previously, Ali Akbar was taught vocal music (which continued alongside training on the *sarod*), supplemented with the study of *tabla*. It

---

[14] Copy of a letter written to his disciple Shri Rebati Ranjan Debnath has been given in appendix.

may be mentioned here that Ali Akbar's first lessons in *tabla* were from his uncle, his father's elder brother Aftabuddin.

In 1936, Baba traveled to Europe with Uday Shankar's dance troupe on a contract for one year as its music director. However, he declined to continue with the troupe for the American part of the tour because of concern for his son Ali Akbar's training. Ustad Allauddin felt that he needed to be in Maihar to guide him properly and that staying away too much could lead the youth's immense talent in undesirable directions in music. The master was more eager for the future career of his son than earning laurels and money from the proposed American tour.

Upon returning to Maihar, Ustad Allauddin Khan adamantly bound Ali Akbar to rigorous schedule of training. He dictated his son to practice day and night. The total hours spent by Ali Akbar Khan on practice at this time varied from fourteen to sixteen hours. Pandit Ravi Shankar also underscores this great fact about Ustad Ali Akbar Khan: "Ali Akbar Khan was born with music in his veins, but it was this constant rigorous discipline and *riaz* (Urdu for "practice") that Baba set for him that has made Ali Akbar Khan one of the greatest instrumentalists alive." Allauddin Khan's tenacious nature and extraordinary energy for hard labor were the basic elements in building up Ali Akbar Khan into one of the greatest musicians of our time.

In his early 20s, Ustad Ali Akbar Khan became the music director of All India Radio in Lucknow. He performed solo programs and composed for the radio-orchestra. About his relationship with his father during this period, Ali Akbar Khan said, "My father's main purpose was to hear me play while he was living in Maihar, because I was always being broadcast. If I played anything wrong, he would come the next day to Lucknow, straight from the train station, tell me to get my *sarod* and listen to me play and correct me."15

While in Lucknow, Ustad Ali Akbar Khan's extensive recording career began its skyrocketing ascent in 1945, when he recorded a series of 78rpm recordings on *sarod* for HMV. Among these is the legendary three-minute spontaneous *raga* creation he named "Chandranandan." *Raga Chandranandan* received a great deal of radio play and became a favorite of his audience. He later recorded a full version of this *raga*.16

Following this, Ali Akbar Khan became the court musician for the maharaja of Jodhpur, where he performed long concerts and composed music for the court orchestra. Unfortunately, the maharaja died in a plane crash in 1948 and, along with the sad death of the king, the post of court musician was no longer.

---

15   "The Dawn of Indian Music in the West" Peter Lavezzoli.

16   *See* Appendix II for Ustad Ali Akbar's own comments about the creation of *Raga Chandranandan*, its aftermath, and his thoughts on new *ragas* in general.

Ustad Ali Akbar Khan then went to Bombay, against the wishes of his father. During this period, he scored for films made both in Bombay and Calcutta, including films by legendary Bengali filmmakers Satyajit Ray and Tapan Sinha. Unknowingly, Baba Allauddin Khan had gone to see the film "Hungry Stones"by Tapan Sinha and loved the score. He inquired as to who this great musician was who scored this film and was more than surprised to find out that it was his son Ali Akbar. Upon knowing this, Baba sent a telegram of forgiveness to his son.

Not long afterwards, Ustad Ali Akbar Khan returned to the stage of performing Indian Classical Music. The legendary violinist Yehudi Menuhin came to hear him in the early 1950s and proclaimed in written and spoken word that Ali Akbar Khan was "an absolute genius." In 1955, Yehudi Menuhin had garnered sponsors and invited Ali Akbar Khan to play a concert in New York City. This began a turn of events that was historic in proportion, with no exaggeration in that statement. In New York, Ustad Ali Akbar Khan recorded what many believe to be the first long-playing record of Indian Classical Music. (It is also thought by some that the great Ustad of shehnai, Bismillah Khan, recorded the first long playing record of Indian Classical Music (in India)). After brother-in-law – and fellow disciple of Allauddin Khan – Pandit Ravi Shankar followed suit in the United States, the popularity of Indian Classical Music took firm hold in the West. Ali Akbar Khan and Ravi Shankar duet concerts became the stuff of historical books, although their careers went in separate directions after a short while.

The most significant event since the time of his training with his legendary father took place in 1967, when Ustad Ali Akbar Khan founded the fully government-accredited"Ali Akbar College of Music"in San Rafael, California. Ali Akbar Khan settled there and focused on making the college a landmark institution in the world for learning Indian Classical Music without popular influences. The college also became a place for touring Indian musicians to make a regular concert stop, and its "music store" is one of the few places in the world from where one can buy quality Indian instruments and accessories for the instruments. The store is also one of the bona fide shops for Indian Classical Music recordings and boasts a large catalog.[17]

The legendary Baba Allauddin Khan's son had also become a legend. Like his great father, Ustad Ali Akbar Khan received the Padma Vibhushan award (the second highest national award in India) in 1989. In 1991, he became the first Indian musician to receive the MacArthur Foundation Award in the United States known as the "genius grant."In 1997, he was given the National Heritage Fellowship Award of the U.S. National Endowment for the Arts.

In June of 2009, the torchbearer of Ustad Allauddin Khan's legacy, Baba's son Ustad Ali Akbar Khan passed away from kidney failure at the age of 87, leaving a

---

[17]   *See* Appendix II for Ustad Ali Akbar Khan's comments on the school.

void in the realm of Indian Classical Music that will be impossible to fill. His sons Aashish and Alam ably continue the lineage on *sarod.*

SHRIMATI ANNAPURNA DEVI

Baba's elder daughter had married into a Muslim family in Dhaka. Although she had learned to sing from her father, her in-laws did not approve of her singing, and her mother-in-law even burned down her *tanpura* (drone instrument) to put a stop to her music. This shocked Allauddin Khan so much that he never encouraged his youngest daughter Annapurna to learn music. But she used to sit and listen to her father and brother very carefully.

One day when Baba was out in the marketplace, she began to sing like her father and amended a piece which Ali Akbar had not picked up correctly. Baba had forgotten to take his purse and came back home to fetch it. But on that day an altogether new sensation was in store for him. There the great master stood, speechless and deeply moved. It was the first time he had heard his daughter Annapurna sing. His great delight was, however, cut short. No sooner had Baba's children Annapurna and Ali Akbar caught his sight, they broke off. Annapurna almost became petrified with fright at the sight of her father, who asked her to come with him to his apartment on the first floor. She could not help giving way to wailing in apprehension of being beaten black and blue by her father. But, to her great surprise and relief, nothing untoward occurred. The Ustad made her sit and wanted her to sing a second time what she had sung a little earlier. With a lot of hesitation and panic, she sang through her tears, weeping all the while. Her performance pleased Ustad Allauddin so much that he patted her back in appreciation and directed her to learn from him regularly from then on. While her elder brother Ali Akbar Khan cultivated *sarod,* she studied the *sitar* and after some time took to *surbahar,* for which she was the most known, and often thought to be peerless on that instrument.

Since childhood, there was tremendous swiftness in her hand. Baba was inspired with her talent. She was taught all of the complex techniques of *been anga* by her father.

Baba was so distraught at the untimely death of his second daughter Jahanara that he once told Annapurna Devi that he would not marry her with any human being, but with music. It was understood that he had imparted all of his advanced knowledge to his extraordinarily talented daughter.

Although she stopped performing publicly in an early stage of her professional career because of personal reasons, Annapurna Devi is recognized by the musicians and connoisseurs in the know as a musician equally as great and of the same stature as her famous brother Ali Akbar Khan. Many well-known artists have come to study with Annapurna Devi and consider her as one of their primary *gurus.* Because of the internet, and the desires of some well wishers, some of her unpublished recordings are becoming available today, and duly astonishing the listeners with her grace, knowledge and expression of *raga*, and breathtaking virtuosity.

GRANDSONS

Baba started imparting lessons to his grandsons Ashish Khan (*sarod*), Dhyanesh Khan (*sarod*) and Shubendra Shankar (*sitar*) from a very early age. When Allauddin Khan taught the boys, he himself followed them on *tabla* and always maintained this fundamental principle that *talim* (training) without *tala* (rhythm) is not complete. When his grandsons played well he would encourage them, saying, "You have won over your grandfather. You will beat even me by your excellent performance I see."

Allauddin Khan taught them strictly, although tactfully. Baba always impressed upon them that they would do well to listen to the old compositions with full attention.

Whenever Allauddin Khan participated in musical conferences or functions, he made it a point to take young Ashish with him for accompaniment on the sarod during his performance. In this way, the young boy learned how to face the audience quite early in his career. Sometimes the trio of Allauddin, Ali Akbar and Ashish played together in conferences demonstrating the excellent combination of three generations of artists.

Baba began teaching Ashish Khan at the age of six. During his sixteen years of training with the Ustad, he was taught techniques both in vocal and instrumental music. His grandson has become a worthy torchbearer of his illustrious grandfather's style.

PANDIT RAVI SHANKAR

Ravi Shankar received his first lesson at the hands of Ustad Allauddin Khan during their foreign itinerary program in Europe. It may be mentioned here that both of them had been included in the touring troupe of Uday Shankar at that time – Baba as the music director and Ravi Shankar, then only in his early teens, as a dancer. Ravi Shankar learned the elements of both vocal and instrumental music. He took up *sitar* as his instrument. Although he was a hard working student and put all his heart in his musical lessons, somehow or other Ustad Allauddin Khan had a feeling that Ravi was not as drawn towards music as to dancing, because he was regularly taking part in rehearsals and performances of the troupe. But the Ustad was convinced that Ravi Shankar had great possibilities to become a master musician. He thought that it was a frittering away of rare energy and aptitude by dancing, when the same ought to have been exclusively devoted to music. He disliked the fact that the boy had a knack of dressing himself foppishly and mixing with the girls of the troupe. He felt that his student should be wholeheartedly devoted only to music just like the sages of ancient days, caring not even for painting, writing and reading, of which the young trainee was very fond. Ustad Allauddin Khan would warn him, "*Ek sadhe sab sadhe, sab sadhe sab jaye*" i.e., the best course for him was to master one subject, namely music, which will eventually lead to his command over so many other subjects. But if he started having too many irons in the fire he would not have even one.

Baba's admonitions to anybody, least of all Ravi Shankar, were not tainted with any real and lasting grudge or grievance. Whatever he criticized in Ravi's goings on was not out of any ill feeling on his part. He truly loved to teach Ravi. The young boy also was conscious of it. It helped him to learn everything quickly and perfectly whenever the maestro seemed soft and kind. Similarly the master's peevishness and ill-humor took all zest out of Ravi and he actually became so crossed as to refuse to pick up anything. The truth about Ravi Shankar was that he had been very touchy and sensitive since his childhood and could never stand a strong dressing down or castigation. As a matter of fact, no one teased him or hurt his sentiments by any rude word.

It so happened that in 1936, during the summer, Uday Shankar's troupe stayed for several months at Dartington Hall, situated in Devonshire of England. The place was beautiful, and expansive and sprawling. Ravi Shankar found himself with ample time for practicing sitar and at the same time obtaining lessons from the Ustad Allauddin Khan. It was here that, for the first time, he practiced in accordance with proper scales and set lessons. Until now, he had cared to play whatever pleasant melodies that occurred to his mind at any flight of fancy. But he spent the whole period at Dartington Hall practicing exercises and compositions with great zeal and concentrated effort. It was over here that Ravi Shankar started having a sort of inspiration for becoming a great master. He felt like dedicating his life to this art. However, in autumn, Baba all of a sudden and unexpectedly had to sail back home to India quite earlier than scheduled. It was for Ravi Shankar a moment of great crisis, he having been torn between two parallel urges. On the one hand, he wanted to get on with dancing as a career and, on the other, there came moments when he longed to become a great instrumentalist. However, Baba had not forgotten to remind him before parting that if he really wanted to master music with his help, he would do well to come to him at his house in the small Maihar town and devote several years to training over there under him. He also reminded him that in so doing he would have to forgo a good deal of the glamor of his artistic career in European surroundings. It was also a fact that Allauddin Khan was not sure whether Ravi's interest in learning music from him was that deep.

Ravi Shankar, however, had learned from Baba about *sitar* playing to such an extent that with a little practice he was in a position to perform on the instrument all alone or solo. Sometimes he actually gave solo performances as part of the program of the troupe. However, after Allauddin Khan's departure from Europe, Shankar had started practicing the *sarod*, which he handled in the orchestra of the troupe.

For sometime *sarod* remained his major preoccupation. He was drawn to the *sarod* because he was deeply moved by Baba's mastery on the instrument and wanted to follow in his footsteps. Baba imparted training to him in *sitar*, and not *sarod*, because when he came into contact with the master, Ravi Shankar had already learned some things on the *sitar*. In 1938 Ravi Shankar sailed for India, and began to live and study in Maihar with Ustad Allauddin Khan. Without anyone's knowledge, and particularly hiding it from his brother Uday Shankar, he had carried on correspondence with Baba. He had been afraid that Uday Shankar might put stop to his dream as he wanted his youngest brother to be a dancer like him, without scattering his attention in the pursuit of vocal or instrumental music beyond a certain point.

Besides being taught individually by Baba, Ravi Shankar was also made to learn and practice in the company of Ali Akbar Khan and Annapurna Devi, the great master teaching them simultaneously in their respective instruments.

It was Baba who first obtained Pandit Ravi Shankar's engagements with the Lucknow Station of the All India Radio, which helped the young and upcoming artist immensely in being fit for future concerts. This throws light on another aspect of Baba's character. He was not only a powerful and musician and an able teacher, but also a man who often went out of his way to come to the assistance of his students in establishing themselves in their careers.

Pandit Ravi Shankar and his illustrious brother-in-law Ustad Ali Akbar Khan, were the two musicians who spearheaded the spreading of Indian Classical Music to the West, and it can be said that it is because of Ravi Shankar and Ali Akbar Khan, Indian Classical Music became a financially viable art on the world scene.

Like his great *guru* Ustad Allauddin Khan and his virtuoso brother-in-law Ustad Ali Akbar Khan, Pandit Ravi Shankar was also awarded the Padma Vibhushan award by the Indian Government.

Pandit Ravi Shankar continues to carry on the tradition of the *Senia Gharana* and the legacy of Baba Allauddin Khan by performing stellar concerts even in his early 90s.

PANDIT TIMIR BARAN BHATTACHARYA

Timir Baran Bhattacharya (known nationally simply as "Timir Baran") was one of Ustad Allauddin's foremost and senior-most disciples. Timir Baran lived at Maihar for a long time and learned *sarod* from the great maestro under his strict care.

Timir Baran had been initially a pupil of Ustad Amir Khan in Calcutta, before becoming the disciple of Ustad Allauddin Khan. Timir Baran remained under the guidance of Amir Khan for about five years. The incident which made him Baba's disciple was an interesting one. Once Allauddin Khan had come to Calcutta to perform a concert which Timir had attended. He was completely taken by Baba's magnificent *sarod* recital. Timir made straight for the house where the master had been staying. He asked Baba to accept him as his disciple. But the *guru* at first refused, saying that Timir lived far away from Maihar; thus it would be impossible for him to teach Timir. The young boy immediately replied that he would go to Maihar if Baba would train him. Timir had also mentioned the name of the Ustad from whom he had been learning at that time. Allauddin Khan gave this information some thought. Eventually Baba had to soften considerably at the stiff insistence and importunity of the young aspirant. The Ustad asked Timir Baran to play him a piece or two of his music at the earliest opportunity. He prepared himself and a program was arranged at the house of Sheetal Mukherjee. Timir performed superbly. Baba was immensely happy with his playing. As Allauddin Khan was a man of noble heart, he pointed out that Timir had already gained a great deal of knowledge from Ustad Amir Khan (Timir Baran's *guru* at the time and to whom he had been like a son), so he might have nothing more to pass on to him. But the young man had been as firm as a rock in his determination to become a disciple of Ustad Allauddin Khan. So at last Baba had to relent, but that also only on the condition that the boy must obtain the consent of his then existing teacher in writing and show it to him. Timir went to the house of Ustad Amir Khan and expressed his wish. Ustad Amir Khan was saddened to hear the news because Timir had been his favorite student. But in the end he gave Timir his permission and the young musician traveled to Maihar to receive further training there from Ustad Allauddin Khan. He was then 20 years old.

Timir Baran was known as a genius. When he came to Maihar, he had already a sound background in his art. His already acquired knowledge and Baba's rigorous training added a new chapter to his career. Due to his hard labor and brilliance, he soon became a favorite of his guru. Timir did tremendous *sadhana* (absorbed practice) there. It was Baba who used to say that if he had to face some mishap, then Timir would take up the training of Ali Akbar, who had been a baby at that time.

From Ustad Allauddin Khan's examples, Timir Baran obtained a thorough grounding in composing and conducting orchestral music. The Maihar Band, a unique handiwork of Baba, was, by and large, instrumental in imbuing Timir with the zeal and ability to arrange orchestral scores. The example of the Maihar Band had struck his imagination to such an extent that he organized an orchestra with the members of his own family in Calcutta as its players.

The well-known pioneer of dance in India, Uday Shankar, was greatly impressed by Timir's *sarod* playing. He took him into his troupe as the music director as well as a soloist. After an all-India tour, his troupe, in which Timir Baran wielded the music conductor's baton, came to Bombay on the way to Europe. Immediately after reaching Bombay, Uday Shankar wrote to Dilip Kumar Roy, one of Timir's admirers:

"I regard myself as lucky in having Timir Baran with me. I have been traveling through India for the last seven months, but was never so much impressed as by his music. He is really wonderful with his *sarod*. When I came to India I never dreamt of a decent Indian orchestra, but Timir Baran's orchestra that lately accompanied my dance in Calcutta made me change my mind. I only hope there will be more parties than that."

Western audiences were thrilled to hear his artistic creations on *sarod*. He was the first musician to introduce *sarod* in Europe. In his days, Timir Baran was the most popular *sarod* player in Bengal. Uday Shankar very much appreciated Timir's musical direction and compositions and entrusted him with the conception and conduction of the entire musical scores for his famous choreographies, such as "*Indira*," "*Gandharva*," "*Marwari Bride*" among others. The artistic brilliance of Uday Shankar's ballets was greatly heightened by Timir Baran's effective musical accompaniment.

It is said that Timir Baran joined Uday Shankar's troupe in a mysterious manner. One morning he left Maihar without breathing a single word about it to Ustad Allauddin Khan or, for that matter, anyone else. He played a sort of truant to tour with Uday Shankar's troupe as its music director. Of course, Baba was taken aback at Timir Baran's sudden and unceremonious parting. The two did not meet for the next 17 years. Nevertheless, the two remarkable musicians, *guru* and disciple, were reconciled in the end.

PANDIT PANNALAL GHOSH

Pannalal Ghosh was a disciple of Ustad Allauddin Khan on the flute, which was not in the usual line of the great master, although the Ustad had also a good grounding in wind instruments. Born on July 31, 1911, in the Barisal district of East Bengal (now Bangladesh), Pannalal Ghosh was interested in pipe playing from a very early age. Very soon he took to the flute. Pannalal Ghosh was considered the first to properly use flute in the interpretation of classical music in all its ramifications and characteristics, including *alapchari, gat, tan, bol*-work in all the *layas* – from *vilambit* to *ati drut*. It is widely accepted that it was Pannalal Ghosh who made the flute fully acceptable and suitable for pure Indian classical music. Before him Gopal Lahiri, brother of Tulsi Lahiri, the celebrated music director of the Gramaphone Company of India, had played classical music on the flute, using particularly the *khyal anga*. But his sudden and premature death put a stop to his pioneering classical way of playing on what was considered a folk instrument. But in the 1940's, Gopal Lahiri's direction on the simple bamboo flute was carried forward in Bengal by Pannalal Ghosh.

Pannalal Ghosh earned country-wide fame by recording his music as well as by direct performance in big functions and conferences. His skill in music was then confined to his achievements as a flute virtuoso of immaculate capability. Gradually Pannalal moved forward into the realm of composition. In this area, the Bombay film industry for sometime provided a very congenial climate for him. Here he gradually got himself elevated to the role of music composer and director. Some of his musical scores brought him immense fame as a very able and imaginative composer. *Basant*, a production of *Filmistan* Company, created a countrywide sensation not so much for its story, acting or other qualities as its gripping and sweet music. For several months at a stretch, it drew full houses in Bombay, Calcutta and many other big and small cities. Its songs became so popular that they were sung even in the remote countryside. But easy fame and money could not keep him tied to Bombay, as he was fired with the ambition of becoming a top-class Indian classical musician with his flute as the medium. On the suggestion of Ravi Shankar, he proceeded to Maihar to sit at the feet of Ustad Allauddin Khan and get training from him in the most intricate and deepest features of classical music. After a few years of training under Baba, Pannalal Ghosh became known as the fountainhead of the "classical North Indian bamboo flute." All flutists following the classical idiom in the North Indian way invariably pay homage to him.

Pannalal Ghosh was a man of imagination and originality. In order to suit his purpose, he remodeled and renovated the ordinary flute into a much bigger and more sophisticated instrument.

His reputation as a classical flutist was not confined to national boundaries only. He traveled overseas and charmed Western audiences as well with his very capable and high-level performances. Unfortunately, his premature death cut short his eventful career. When he was working as the conductor of the National Orchestra in the All India Radio in Delhi he fell ill with lung trouble and succumbed to a fatal end sometime afterwards.

MRS. SHARAN RANI (BACKLIWAL)

Smt. Sharan Rani was one of the leading musicians of India in the 20th century. As an eminent *sarod* player, she received national and international recognition not only due to her sheer virtuosity but also because of the original style she had devoloped.

She achieved distinction both as a composer and a performer. Her name became synonymous with *sarod* and as such she was often called "*Sarod* Rani" (*Sarod* Queen). Born in 1929, she took to dance and music in early childhood and was acclaimed as a child-prodigy, having given her first public performance at the age of seven. She was on the concert stage for several decades. Her whole life was dedicated to the cause of music. She took her training under Ustad Allauddin Khan and Ustad Ali Akbar Khan. She was trained in classical Indian dance under Achhan Maharaj (*Kathak*), Guru Nabha Kumar Sinha (*Manipuri*) and also studied classical vocal music. Her pupils include both Indians and non-Indians.

PANDIT NIKHIL BANERJEE

One of Baba's most illustrious disciples was Nikhil Banerjee. He was introduced to Baba by Birendra Kishore Roy Chowdhury as a keen aspirant for *sitar* music. He received his training in the instrument from the great master at Maihar for several years. After Baba's demise, his rigorous training continued under the guidance of Ali Akbar Khan and Annapurna Devi. As a virtuoso of commendable skill, Nikhil Banerjee gained eminence and praise both within and outside India. His performances on the *sitar* in Europe and America received he highest accolades from the circles of scholars and music lovers alike. An absolute master of the instrument, he passed away at the early age of 55 in the year 1986. His dedication to riyaz on the instrument was unparalleled, and was demonstrated in performance after performance of high art and flawless presentation.

USTAD BAHADUR KHAN

Bahadur Khan was born in his ancestral home in Bangladesh (then East Bengal) in 1931. His father Ustad Ayat Ali Khan, the youngest brother of Ustad Allauddin Khan, was a master of *surbahar*. Although vastly endowed with expertise in Indian classical music, Ustad Ayat Ali was not eager for publicity and popularity; he was as modest as his elder brother. On being requested by the poet Rabindranath Tagore to join the Vishwa-Bharati at Shantinketan as a member of the musical staff, Ustad Ayat Ali Khan agreed to take the post.

Bahadur Khan was initiated into music at the hands of his father Ayat Ali Khan when he was only five years of age. Two years later he began to take lessons from his uncle Ustad Allauddin Khan. This was followed with his two decade-long apprenticeship at Maihar – a period marked by uncommon devotion to music and the most strenuous *riaz* or practice. When he became a concert artist on his own, he was considered to be amongst the most accomplished instrumentalist of the time.

Bahadur Khan imbibed all the peculiarities and characteristics of the *Senia Gharana*, to which he, by training, came to belong. His *alapchari* as well as *gatkari* was marked by imagination and polished skill. His music not only had melodic appeal but was also characterized by accuracy of technique, conception and interpretation. His deft *gamaks*, *meends* and firm strokes all combined to create an environment of sweetness and sublimity. His treatment of the *ragas* was emotional and presented with measured rhythm and melodic grace.

Bahadur Khan's music was based on the techniques of Ustad Allauddin Khan and of the *Senia Gharana*. Based on *Dhrupad anga* (approach) and the style of the *beena*, Bahadur Khan's *sarod* playing sparkled in melody and rhythm alike. Sometimes his expositions of pensive and melancholic tunes and notes produced a powerful impression upon the minds of his listeners who found it difficult to resist tears. One of his many grand innovations was the exquisite combination of three beautiful *ragas: Rab Bhairav, Rupvati* and *Hindol-lalit*, which used to turn the atmosphere in the places of performance into a veritable dreamland.

VASANT RAI

The eminent sarodist Pandit Vasant Rai, born in 1942, first learned Hindusthani Classical music from his older brother Shri Kantilal Barot. Recognized as a prodigy at a young age, Pandit Rai was accepted in his middle teens by Ustad Allauddin Khan to be his disciple. From 1956 to 1966 Pandit Rai went through rigorous and complete training under the guidance of the great Ustad in his home in Maihar. In 1959, Pandit Rai began teaching at the behest of his guru at the Allauddin Khan college of music. After some years, satisfied that the stellar disciple was ready to be an artist in his own right, Allauddin Khansaheb encouraged Pandit Vasant Rai to "spread his wings" and travel to different parts of India and the world and perform concerts under his own name.

Pandit Rai launched his career in 1967 as a top artist for All India Radio. He then traveled to the United States in the following year, and founded the *Alam School of Indian Classical Music* in New York City. There he dedicated himself to teaching hundreds of students, notable among them were Collin Wacott, Don Cherry, George Harrison and many other rock and jazz personalities of the era, as well as those exclusively interested in pursuing Hindusthani Classical Music as well. It was during this time that the maestro was signed by Vanguard Records and released his first recording in 1972, followed by many others.

Pandit Vasant Rai was known for playing peaceful and extensive alaps (movements without a percussion instrument) in the Dhrupad style (the oldest and most orthodox framework), crisp articulation, and tremendous command over the most complex of rhythms. Panditji toured extensively throughout Europe and had many students worldwide.

Sadly, at the age of 42, Pandit Vasant Rai was stricken with aggressive end stage prostate cancer, and passed on within three months of his diagnosis. His last concert was at the prestigious Carnegie Hall in New York City, one week before his death. After the concert, he was immediately medicated intravenously following the performance, demonstrating his love of music and overcoming barriers to continue playing. On March 8, 1985, he passed from this mortal plane, leaving a huge void in the world of Indian Classical Music.

Chapter 8

IN HIS ILLUSTRIOUS GRANDSON USTAD ASHISH KHAN'S WORDS

"THE CONTRIBUTIONS OF my grandfather cannot be studied in a few words. For one thing, he gave new life to the domain of Indian classical instrumental music. Hitherto it had been kept limited within the families of great old masters. They never teach anybody outside the circle of their own blood relations, such as their own sons and daughters. But my grandfather was of a different brand, after learning from the old masters in his early days, he lavishly made use of his learning to make his house an open-door institution for just anybody to come in and learn from him. He did not care whether his pupil possessed talent or not," says Ustad Ashish Khan, the stellar *sarodist* and grandson of Ustad Allauddin Khan.

Ustad Ashish Khan goes a little further to elucidate on the dissemination of his grandfather's musical developments, both adopted and self-evolved, not only all over India but in the world at large. It clearly shows how absolutely liberal and ungrudging he had been in regard to his art, for which he did yeoman's service over several decades. Ashish Khan says, "Today his (Allauddin Khan's) name and music have been popularized by his many disciples all over the world. His achievements, like the combination of the techniques of *been* and *rabab* with that of *sarod*, all based on *Dhrupad anga* (form), can be traced to Mian Tansen and other *Senis*. We are known as *Senis* (belonging to the *Senia Gharana*). My grandfather further enriched the *Seni* technique or the *tal* and the depth of the *raga, alap, jod, jhala* and all other nuances which were never used in so much detail before as my grandfather had done."

Ustad Allauddin Khan had established many original techniques and began trends which would prevail in classical music, especially in regards to the *sarod*. His original and independent contribution to music would give one the impression that the master might have created and developed a particular *gharana* of his own. On this point, Ashish Khan says, "Although we have not given the name *gharana* to grandfather's styles and techniques, people, of course, call these as pertaining to the *Maihar Gharana*. But basically we are all of the *Senia Gharana*. However, it is true that my grandfather's contribution cannot just be measured with this *gharana* only. But what I am trying to say is that we have not given any name to our *gharana;* we are just known as *Senia Gharana*. To illustrate this point, *Dhrupad* is our roots and mixture of the *beenkar* and the *rabab* style of playing characterizes our music based on *Dhrupad anga.*"

Ashish Khan continues, "My grandfather's way of teaching was oral. That is our tradition. He used to play sometime on his *sarod*, but mostly even while playing, he used to stop and start just singing. I also used to imitate his vocal music. That means it is known as an oral tradition and a *Dhrupad* style of singing."

Regarding his grandfather's emphasis on discipline, Ashish Khan says, "He was definitely a short-tempered person, but the thing was, it was a blessing for us all, because with his strict discipline and with his temperament we had to devote ourselves earnestly to training. He would be scolding and even beating us. My own experience is that we all benefited by it in our training. Though he used to love me very much, I never had that type of relationship which usually a grandfather and a grandchild have. Definitely I knew that he was very loving and loved me most, but his strict discipline and his scolding and beating me during training made me quite scared of him and sometimes I used to keep away from him. All our brothers and sisters got the same type of treatment."

He concludes, "Whatever I have learned from Dadu (grandfather) I play. One can notice different styles in my playing; most of them, of course, are my grandfather's. Some styles are also of my father's, Uncle's (Ravi Shankar), and Aunt's (Annapurna Devi), because I have learned from them all. So I want to play according to all their styles. Of course the root of all these is of my grandfather's making."[18]

---

[18] From writer's conversation with Ustad Ashish Khan.

Chapter 9

CONCLUSION

L OOKING AT THE spectacular career of Ustad Allauddin Khan, who was one of the most outstanding causes of the Indian musical renaissance, one can say without the least hesitation that he had to his credit the most remarkable achievements in the field of this art. Many musical geniuses, preceding and following him, although highly successful as individual exponents, were not able to leave a legacy that would benefit musicians and music lovers in a world-wide scale, mostly because of a lack of vision or the tradition of secrecy. Baba had been a remarkable exception.

Firstly, his attitude to the art of music was more spiritual than sensuous. In his perception the highest aesthetics was on spiritual. Baba's motto was:

Pujat koti phalang strotram
Strotat koti phalo japah:
Japat koti phalam ganam
Ganat parataram nahi

(Meaning: A sacred verse flows from many a worship, from many sacred verses come the meditative chanting of mantras, from copious chanting blossoms out music and there is nothing beyond music.)

Secondly, he not only delved as deep as possible into the secret realms of this art, but also took great pains to build up a large institution which would turn out skillful players and virtuosos in a never-ending stream to carry forward the torch lit by him through years of strenuous and selfless endeavor. Pandit Ravi Shankar has rightly said:

"Baba himself believes he is well over a hundred years old, and his centenary has already been marked. His true age is not known, because records have not been kept, but what does it matter if he is over a hundred or nearing a hundred? What he has accomplished in his lifetime many others could not do if they had three hundred years to live. He is respected and well regarded by everyone, including the most orthodox Hindu Brahmins, as a rishi, responsible for safeguarding traditions, for developing, teaching, and passing on to disciples the art of music."[19]

In keeping with his world outlook based on a synthesizing and unprejudiced approach to human beings and things, his musical conceptualization and techniques were also characterized by the most progressive and dynamic inventions and creativity. At the same time, he did not look down upon the rich traditions of the Indian classical music. He absorbed himself fully in the heritage. However, his passion was to further develop and enrich the traditional concepts and techniques through original and creative contributions. In his personal life he had been as pious as unorthodox. Being a Muslim, he also had great respect for other faiths, particularly Hinduism. He only made sure that everyone and everything about him remained above all narrow-mindedness and neglect. As Ravi Shankar has put it, "And so, even though his family was Muslim, Baba knew all the ways of Hindus and was well acquainted with their customs and ceremonies. Later, he was to follow a way of life that was a beautiful fusion of the best of both Hinduism and Islam."[20]

In the same way, Baba never allowed himself to be short-sighted and high-nosed in regards to any musical direction, traditional or modern, Oriental or Occidental. He was a master of synthesis. In his own life Allauddin Khan epitomized the co-mingling of different and diverse trends and ideas. He did not hesitate to pull down the barriers between the various branches of music, between instrumental and vocal music, between one instrument and another. We have already discussed how all his pupils, learning instrumental music at his hands, were required strictly to habituate themselves in the vocal art as well. Likewise, he brought about a fine blending between the *sarod* and the *beena* style of playing. Be it *sitar* or *surbahar* or *sarod* or any other instrument, all crude and superficial compartmentalization of one of these instruments from another lost their significance. He realized through his deep knowledge and keen perception that there was a very pronounced harmony and similarity amongst the different types of instrumental music.

At the bottom of all of his super-human achievements existed decades-long struggles. Ustad Allauddin Khan put in no fewer than almost four decades of

---

[19] "My Music, My Life" by Pandit Ravi Shankar.

[20] "My Music, My Life" by Pandit Ravi Shankar.

extraordinary *sadhana* or strenuous practice for the acquisition of the utmost knowledge and skill in his beloved art. One really wonders, looking back at all those difficult and dreary years of his training period, how he could have sustained his zeal and patience so long in the teeth of the heaviest odds in all forms. He was equipped with the great virtue of detachment. He was above all petty considerations of life and ardently believed in honesty of purpose and tireless perseverance and labor.

Baba believed in the wise maxim:

Karmanyeva adhikaraste
ma faleshu kadachana

That is to say his motto was to go on endeavoring sincerely and conscientiously without bothering about the outcome of his efforts. In this way, he could accomplish the super-human feat of persisting for decades on end in order to attain complete mastery over his art.

Ustad Allauddin Khan's greatness was not confined to the field of music only. True, as far as artists and connoisseurs were concerned, his place of work and adoption, Maihar, turned into a hotly sought-after place of pilgrimage. But then Maihar was a place of pilgrimage to countless others as well – especially to people in the surrounding regions. For his unassuming and saintly nature he was held in great reverence and love alike by the common people far and near. Whoever had heard of him, not to speak of those who had actually enjoyed his immediate presence, made it a part of his life to pay him a visit and ask for his blessing. They loved to hear him talk about life and the very common things of the world, and relate these all to eternal truths and human ideals. Most of all they were impressed by his plain living, high thinking philosophy and humanist considerations. He was one who actually practiced whatever good things he might have counseled others to do. In this respect, it is pertinent to quote Pandit Vinay Chandra Maudgalya, Principal of the Gandharva Mahavidyalaya in New Delhi. He has said, "I was fortunate enough to be at Maihar and I think it was my pilgrimage. Ustad Allauddin Khan was a great saint."[21]

Baba's exceptional mastery over the various branches of music, along with his qualities of head and heart, brought him name, fame, adoration and honor in plenty. But being himself the very image of modesty and humility, he never allowed his head to be turned. He remained simple and innocent, devoid of the slightest tinge of pride or arrogance. Dr. (Mrs.) Sumati Mutatkar describes this aspect in the great maestro's character, comparing him to a stooping tree, laden with fruit from one end to another, as follows:

---

[21] From a talk the writer had with Pandit Vinay Chandra Maudgalya.

Namanti phaleno vrikshah
Namanti gunino janah
Shushkang kashthang cha murkhascha
Vhidhayte na tu nammyate

However, with all his modesty and good-natured character, Baba never bowed before injustice, but would stand up against it relentlessly.

Having been born at a time when the cultural renaissance movement in Bengal and the rest of India had been at its zenith, Allauddin Khan deeply breathed in the fresh air of progressivism and urge for national identification, on the one hand, and, on the other, a humanist world outlook, based on the ideals of freeing man from all manner of bondage, material and spiritual, where exploitation by man would be a thing of the past. Loyal to his fellow human beings, Baba was also moved with burning love for the holy motherland, for those groaning and writhing in poverty and misery, ignorance and backwardness, as if institutionalized by 200 years of British exploitation and rule. Although he had not been actively connected with the anti-imperialist struggle for liberation, he was full of sympathy for that great cause. He was sincerely respectful to all leaders and luminaries in the political and cultural spheres of the country and of the world at large. He held Mahatma Gandhi in high esteem and he himself always used a white *khadi* (pure cotton) "Gandhi cap" on his head. Baba was also full of reverence for the poet Tagore, Beethoven and several other great men who had contributed richly to the enrichment of human culture and civilization.

Simple and chaste in his personal thoughts and habits, Ustad Allauddin Khan greatly prized and respected those virtues in whomever he might have discerned these. A person's character was held in high esteem by him, irrespective of age or sex, cast or creed, language or race.

Allauddin Khan was not a petty-minded ethno-centric nationalist. His patriotism blended into a broad world vision. His liberal-mindedness can also be gaged from some his habits. He never cared to see the right-hand portion of a name – the surname – which he considered to be a symbol of narrowness, as it indicated the caste or creed of the person concerned. He also told others to develop this habit of concerning themselves with the left-hand side of a name which gives only the forename of a particular individual without restricting or connoting him to any small category. It had been already shown how he aspired after Hindu-Muslim unity and a healthy synthesis of all faiths and creeds. It was also unusual that an inspired and creative artist like him could be so punctilious about keeping his engagements and doing things to the exact hour, minute and second. Baba was punctual and wanted all those who came in contact with him also to follow his example. It may be mentioned here that his regulated daily routine of life helped him tremendously in keeping himself in good health and spirits as well as maintain his usual activities almost till the last hours of his long life. He was always moving with the times and never straggled or slid back. Perhaps it was in the very nature of the time for great minds like him to march ahead with the age, in tune with the newer hopes and aspirations of the new times. On this point, he can be compared with his contemporary, poet Rabindranath Tagore, who also disliked to fall back and always kept himself abreast of the needs of the age, so as to march forward to progress, shoulder to shoulder with all others, including the youngest of the youths. Allauddin Khan's ever-forward-looking and progressive outlook upon life and things did not sever him from his moorings in the existing setup where there was the right blending of the old and the new. With deep gratitude to the ancient heritage, he was sincerely attached to his old associations and memories. He used to say: "*Puran katha jagaye dere / Nutan hoe uthuk bhese.*" (Meaning: Awaken the ancient thoughts and let them rise up in the ever-newness of the present.)

Baba always labored under a sense of extreme indebtedness to anyone from whom he had happened to receive anything of any kind, even a smile or a sweet word, a glass of water or a cup of tea. He made it his motto to be thankful. As he said: "If anybody has treated you to a glass of water, you must return it with a lot of honey."[22]

Ustad Allauddin Khan was not only grateful throughout his life to his *guru* Wazir Khan, but he also held an infinitely deep sense of attachment and fealty towards the *gharana* or the school, the *Senia*, to which he came to belong through his teacher. His remarkable esteem for the *Senia Gharana* of Ustad Wazir Khan also found expression in his getting his son Ustad Ali Akbar Khan initiated as a disciple of Ustad Dabir Khan, a grandson of Ustad Wazir Khan. He had Ali Akbar go through the *ganda*-tying ceremony at the hands of Ustad Dabir Khan. This should be understood in the background of the fact that it was Ustad Allauddin Khan himself that trained Ustad Ali Akbar Khan in music entirely.

Baba had a great sense of humor as well. Seemingly grave and reserved, he had a knack for humor which was innocent and never derogatory to anybody.

It was no wonder then that he commanded respect as well as love not only from his children, relations and countless disciples, but from all. It is, therefore, in the rightful place of things that the late lamented saintly master lives as ever before in his multi-faceted achievements and contributions to the cause of the development and glory of the art that had been so dear to him. Undoubtedly, the little seed that Ustad Allauddin Khan sowed many years ago has grown into a gigantic tree in full blossom. He lives in his creations. He lives in the achievements of his worthy disciples.

Ustad Allauddin Khan was a total musician of sublime emotions and he had an ardent thirst for knowledge in whatever instrument upon which he might have cared to lay his hands. It was not that he wanted to be a master of all and to achieve

---

22   From writer's talks with Shri Rebati Ranjan Debnath.

more fame or monetary gain. As already mentioned, he was very sentimental and emotional and thus he expressed his different types of emotions and thoughts through different kinds of instruments. He may be called a real researcher in this field. He worked tremendously to pave the way for future generations of musicians and music lovers.

Baba's anger was child-like. It did not harm anyone. It was an echo from his life-long struggle to attain superb mastery over the art. It was like an outburst of his long pent-up agonies and yearnings for perfect melody, harmony and rhythm.

Now it would be certainly an injustice if a writer does not bring in the limelight the leading force behind this great musician Ustad Allauddin Khan, and she is Shrimati Madan Manjari (Allauddin Khan's wife), known to many simply as "Ma." It is quite difficult to draw a picture of her great contribution. She was indeed an ideal wife, an ideal mother and a skilled housewife. She may be compared with Kasturba Gandhi. It is widely accepted that Gandhiji would not have achieved what he did without the help and inspiration from his wife, Kasturba. So it was with Baba. Shrimati Madan Manjari or Ma, as she was called affectionately by his disciples, took the greatest care in looking after their comforts. It was she who used to cook for them all and when they felt some sort of trouble in their hands after practicing, she administered herbs to ease their suffering. Ma had a very sharp eye to save Baba's disciples, who were like her own children, from the anger of her husband. It was due to her carefulness and dutifulness that Allauddin Khan maintained perfect health. And he was one of the rare masters who performed in high form even in his ninetics.

Ma helped Baba in maintaining regularity in life in every sense. Baba himself used to praise this great lady and out of affection and love towards her. He dedicated one of his new musical creations in her name – *Raga Madan Manjari*. Baba also named his house in Maihar after her, calling it "Madina Bhavan." In this connection, Smt. Sharan Rani said, "Ma was really a Shakti (divine force) behind Baba. Behind Baba her contributions are also enormous."[23]

FINAL THOUGHTS

In view of the exceptionally high order of tenacity and arduousness needed for mastery in Indian Classical Music, and also in view of the intricate nature of its nuances which are not necessarily appreciated by the lay public, the future of this branch of the Muses may naturally appear bleak. It had actually been falling into oblivion before the advent of some very talented instrumental masters such as Ustad Allauddin Khan. It is due to their fight against almost impossible odds, both in the industry and in one's personal artistic aims, and their ultimate triumph in

---

[23] From writer's conversation with Smt. Sharan Rani (Backliwal).

both areas – as is exemplified by Allauddin Khan's journey – that the instrumental musical renaissance was able to take place and even today, 3 ½ decades after Baba's passing, continues to thrive.

This valiant missionary and pioneer in the field of Indian Classical music forever bade good bye to this world in 1972, leaving behind a legacy that was further propagated by his landmark disciples and will continue for generations to come.

Bibliography

PART I

1. *The Art of Music*, Eleventh Impression, 1950, C. Hubert H. Parry; published by Routledge & Kegan Paul, Limited., Broadway House: 68-74 Carter Lane, E.C. 4., London – J. Curwen & Sons Ltd.

2. *Glimpses of Indian Music*, First Edition 1959, Vani Bai Ram; Published by Kitab Mahal (W.D.) Private Ltd.

3. *Musicians of India*, Harendra Kishore Roy Chowdhury. India.

4. *Hindustani Sangeete Tansener Sthan*, (in Bengali), Birendra Kishore Roy Chowdhury; published by Bireshwar Bagchi, Gauripur, Mymensingh, India.

5. *Ustad Allauddin Khan And His Music*, First Edition 1979, Jotin Bhattacharya; published by B.S. Shah Prakashan, 1183 Bankore Naka, Ahmedabad – 380001 – India.

6. *Sangeet Prasanga* (in Bengali), June 1980, Rubarak Hussain; published by Al Mahamood, Director-in-Charge, Department of Research and Publications, Bangladesh Shilpakala Academy, Shengunbagicha, Ramna, Dacca-2, Bangladesh.

7. *Amar Katha* (in Bengali), Ustad Allauddin Khan, an interview taken and narrated by Shubhomay Ghosh; published by Anand Publishers, Pvt. Ltd., 45 Beniatola Lane, Calcutta 9, India.

8. *My Music, My Life*, Ravi Shankar; published by Vikas Publications, New Delhi, India.

9. *Ustad Allauddin Khan*, Rajendra Shankar; published by Kinnara Publications, Bombay, India.

10. *The Music of Hindustan*, A.H. Fox Strangeways; published by Oxford Press, at the Clarendon Press; first Published in 1914. Reprinted lithographically at the University Press, Oxford, U.K., from sheets of the First Edition, 1965.

11. *The History of Music*, Cecil Gray; published by Kegal Paul, French, Trubner and Co. Ltd., London, U.K.; and Alfred A. Knopf, New York, U.S.A.; Second Edition (corrected and revised) reprinted in 1945.

12. *Music of India*, Willard and Jones; published by Anil Gupta for Susil Gupta (India), Private Ltd., 23/3-c Galiff Street, Calcutta-4, India.

13. *Ustad Allauddin Khan,* Chitta Ranjan Prakashi; published in "Indraprastha" (Bengali Magazine), New Delhi, India.

14. *Uday Shankar*, Shudha Banjan Mukhopadhyay; published in "Desh" (Bengali Weekly), Calcutta, India.

15. *Sanchayita* (in Bengali), Rabindra Nath Tagore; published by Vishwa Bharati Grantha Bibhag, 5 Dwaraka Nath Tagore Lane, Calcutta-7, India.

16. *Rag Anurag*, Ravi Shankar; published in "Desh" (Bengali Weekly), Calcutta, India.

17. *Malaya, Part I* (in Bengali), Manmohan Dutta; published by Sudhir Chandra Dutta, Ananda Ashram, Satmore, Comilla, Bangladesh.

18. *Srimadbhagvat Gita*, 10th Edition, (in Bengali), annotated by Jagadish Chandra Ghosh; published by Anil Chandra Ghosh, Presidency Library, 15 College Square, Calcutta-13, India.

Though not quoted from, the following books and magazines were consulted by the writer:

1. *The Lives of Great Musicians* and *The Evolution of Songs and Lives of Great Musicians,* S. Bandopadhyay.

2. *Khusro Tansen Tatha Anya Kalakar* (Hindi), Sulochana Brihaspati.

3. *Indian Music, with an Introduction on Indian Musical Theory and Instruments,* Alain Danielou.

4. *Listening to the Hindustani Music* Chetan Karnani.

5. *Music Profiles,* Susheela Misra.

6. *Great Musicians of India,* Dolly Rizvi.

7. *Hindustan Sangeeter Itihas* (Bengali), Birendra Kishore Roy Chowdury and Profulla Kumar Das.

8. *Great Musicians,* P. Sambamoorthy.

9. *Surgam, An Introduction to Indian Music,* Vishnudas Shirali.

10. *The Torchbearer of Indian Music: Maharshi Vishnu Digambar Paluskar,* Ham Avatar "Veer."

11. *Sadhak – Silpir Antim Sayan,* Robin Ghosh; published in "Desh" (Bengali Weekly), Calcutta.

12. *Tripura Theke Maihar,* interview recorded by Shubhomay Ghosh; published in "Ananda Bazar Patrika" (Bengali Daily), Calcutta.

13. *Alapchari Allauddin,* Sunit Ghosh; published in "Ananda Bazar Patrika" (Bengali Daily), Calcutta.

14. *Maestro who Imparts a Tradition,* Anees Jung; published in "The Hindustan Times," August 27, 1972.

15. *The Senia Gharana of Rampur,* Birendra Kishore Roy Chowdhury; published in the Journal of the *Sangeet Natak Akademi,* New Delhi.

16. *Sangeet Sadhak Allauddin Khan,* Shantideb Ghosh; published in "Ananda Bazar Patrika" (Bengali Daily), Calcutta.

17. *Sangeet* (Hindi Fortnightly), April 1976.

18. *Shaiva Vani* (Bengali Monthly).

19. *Sharan Rani Felicitation Volume,* Sharan Rani Abhinandan Samaroh Samiti, New Delhi.

20. *Bhaijee Pandit Vinay Chandra Maudgalya, Shasthipurti Abhinandan,* Vinay Chandra Maudgalya; published by Hirak Jayanti Satkar Samiti.

21. *Ustad Allauddin Khan,* Madan Lal Vyas; published in "Sangeet" (Hindi Fortnightly), December, 1972, Hathras, U.P., India.

22. *Report of the Second All India Music Conference,* Delhi, December 14th to 17th, 1918.

23. *Report of the Fourth All India Music Conference,* Lucknow, 1925.

24. *The Discovery of India: A Ballet,* based on Jawaharlal Nehru's book of the same name and presented by India Renaissance Artists.

25. *Indian Music and Mian Tansen,* Birendra Kishore Roy Chowdhury; published by Krishna Kali Bhattacharya, General Secretary, "Gouripur Music Trust."

Appendices

Appendix I

LETTERS

Maihar
18-5-56

Kalyanbar

I have to work very hard; many students have gathered from outside; it almost turns my head going on training them all and so I sort of forget everything else. My health is not going well for the last 5/6 months; I am suffering a lot from gout. Everyday I have to get an injection; I can move about, but I feel a pain always in the right leg and loin and right hand, for these I am in considerable trouble; there is no need to worry, God will do good. The college opens on the first. I have to coach the Band and college and private boy and girl students for eight hours; even after this I have to labor with boy and girl students from outside, for these reasons I have to spend my time with considerable difficulty. I am now 90 years old; my health cannot cope with all these labors. Your Ma (mother) is physically well. She has become old, so has considerable weakness. All of you accept our blessings and convey these to the grandsons and granddaughters. I am so so. I hope for your welfare.

Yours,
Allauddin

Maihar
9-6-57
Madhya Pradesh

Kalyanbar

I do not accept anything from my disciples. Do I not understand how you are bringing up the grandsons and granddaughters with so much difficulty – earning money with the sweat of your brow? For this reason I am pained to see that you have spent money to send me these articles. The eldest granddaughter is now quite grown up. She has to be given in marriage to a suitable bridegroom. Put aside money from this very moment for this purpose. I could not go to Pakistan [Bangladesh was then East Pakistan]. For the last six months Maihar has turned into a desert land without water. It has become difficult to have grass for feed for the cows and calves. Your mother and your nephew Amaresh are here. I wonder to whom I shall leave them. For these reasons I could not go to my birthplace. Recently a program covering July 19th, 20th and 21st has come from Shilong. Fulfilling these three arrangements I shall go to my birthplace. They will pay me two thousand rupees. Make arrangements for me to take that money to Pakistan. I have made up my mind to go. If meanwhile it rains, I can go, free from all sorts of worry. If they do not make arrangements for me to carry money to Pakistan then I shall go via Agartala. I shall go to your elder brother and it will be well if he can make arrangements to carry the money. Write to your brother about it so that he can make arrangements if I go. Accept your mother's blessing. We are so so. Write to me about your welfare.

Yours,
Baba

Maihar
5-4-60

Kalyanbar

Shriman Baba Rebati I have learned all matters from your letter. I pray to Gracious God:"May He keep you happy." It is impossible for me to inform you when your Ma (mother) will come back. I think I have to spend my last years in the same way as I spent the first part of my life. I bow to the will of Gracious God and I shall remain as He will keep me. I have sent the younger grandsons to Calcutta to study there. The younger grandsons are not very inclined towards music, so I have sent them away to pursue their studies. Your mother being unable to stay without them, I have sent her also. You rest assured that your Ma did not go away feeling angry with me. I have to do much work at Maihar. It's concerned with training and education; I spend my time very happily. Do not harbor any kind of worry whatsoever about me. I am all right. Tender my blessing to Bauma [daughter-in-law] with the name Jagat Mata [Mother of the Universe], conveyed to me from the Himalaya Mountains. You and Bauma chant this name, which will be for your good. Do not neglect the Divine Mother's name, mind you; otherwise it will ruin you. The name is like this –

Ma Ambika Mahamaya
Ma Ambika Mahamaya
Ma Ambika Mahamaya

Convey Divine Mother's name also to Shriman Ravi Shankar and Shrimati Ma Annapurna. Convey Divine Mother's name also to Shriman Ravi Shankar and Shrimati Ma Annapurna. Convey it also to Shriman Pannalal Ghosh. He is also a devoted son of Gracious God.

I am so so. I wish your well being.

Yours,
Baba

Post script: I received the name, which is Mother's gift, two days after I prayed. Believe me that Mother sent it on a postcard, written in Her own hand. The address has been mentioned as from the Himalayas only. At the end of the letter it was written: "Your well-wisher."

Divine Mother has commanded me to propagate this name. For this reason offer this name to all my beloved ones.

Hari Om

Kalyanbar,

Shriman Baba Rebati, all of you, accept my blessings of Vijaya. I pray to Mother Bhagawati – may she keep all of you hale and hearty! You wrote to your Ma* that you would come along with my grandson, I do not know why did you not come. Hope you are all well by the Grace of God. My work has now increased substantially and seems to be without end. I do not get any time even to write a reply when I receive a letter. I also do not have anyone with me whom I may ask to write for me. Make me happy by writing to me from time to time about your well being.

Convey my *adab* [salutation] to the revered Ashfaq Hussain Sahib. I feel like spending the last days of my life in Arab lands. I will be able to attend the Haj every year. Ascertain from Ashfaq Hussain Sahib with a request on behalf of me, whether there are any possibilities for assistance for going there, for board and lodging and whether there can be arrangements made over there, under the supervision of the Government, for visiting the holy Mecca, the holy Medina, Jerusalem, the holy Baghdad, Ka'abakhan and such other places. If I get radio engagements from there occasionally, then I need not obtain Government help to meet my expenses. It will do if only through the blessing and beneficent care of *Khuda* [God] I can find residential accommodation either in Jeidah or Metta. Do not disclose it to anybody else. I have suffered from troubles throughout my life and have not been able to feel happy or peaceful. My heart and soul want to go on a pilgrimage. You are my God-son, so I have appealed to you. I have none else but you to speak all about it to and get help from. Try and see if you can do anything. Do this work which a son ought to. If luck favors, go I must. I am so so. I hope for the welfare of you all.

Your God-father
Allauddin

If it is settled, then I shall have to take a small-sized instrument – *sarod* – with me.

"Ma" – Shrimati Madan Manjari, Ustad Allauddin Khan's wife

This Appendix contains English translations of letters originally written in Bengali by Ustad Allauddin Khan to the author's father Shri Rebati Ranjan Debnath. The scans of the original letters in Bengali are on pages 89-94.
Translated by: Shri Ganendra Chandra Dhar

Appendix II

USTAD ALI AKBAR KHAN'S ASSESSMENT

MY FATHER STUDIED music for over forty years. He learned not only from one teacher. He wanted to learn the right kind of music from one, but he used to go to many teachers. Because he was so thoroughly talented, every teacher liked to tell him after six months: "Look here, I have taught you everything and I have nothing more to teach you." He would submit, "It was not enough for me, I did not come only for this." Then they gave him suggestions to approach other kinds of teachers. This teacher, that teacher and still another. With my father, it happened like that. He learned two hundred kinds of instruments. And then at last he found what he wanted in his life. He spent his whole life to learn, practice and research.

He was never angry with me regarding music, as he himself sometimes used to tell others that from time to time he got nervous when it came to teaching me, because whatever he played or whatever he said, he always felt that I already had known those things. And that was, of course, my great blessing from him. The point is that he always felt like that, but he was never angry with me and I never got any kind of punishment from him from childhood until now. Still, every night I learned from him, because every night I see him in my dream and still I am learning from him many new ragas. The ragas I composed are not mine, but his own. I simply learn those things.

My father invented *Raga Madan Manjari*. "Madan" or "Madina" is my mother's name. He composed it for his wife. I composed it for my mother. The difference is between the scales and moods only. All the rest are similar.

As it is there are already around 75,000 *ragas*, and after that it is not possible to compose many more. Any new *ragas* cannot but be combinations of those ragas I can make or arrange. I tried to make something, to bring about the different moods and that kind of thing. Recently I have been working on *Madan Manjari*. Like *Chandranandan*, you see, actually I did not think about anything at the time of the recording in Bombay. On the request of a producer, my friend Mr. Jyoti, who asked me to play something new, I composed *Chandranandan*, which was recorded. I played in those times when the recording used to be only for three minutes. I played that one. And then it was played back and everyone liked it and then we thought about the name and we all discussed and I said all right, let us give it the name of *Chandranandan*. And then the record came out, and also wherever I performed people used to ask me to play *Chandranandan* and I could not remember what I had done. And then I had to buy my record and start playing, it; and I started learning it, and that took me five years to learn myself what I composed, and still I am learning that one. I think it takes twelve years to master any kind of *raga*. My way of teaching is the same as my father's. Actually Baba used to get angry if somebody could not learn. Anybody can be like that. But sometimes I get angry also with those people like Nikhil Banerjee, who learned from me. If they do not play rightly, then, of course, I get upset. Not in the same way of my father but from inside. But I always try not to lose my temper, because losing one's temper is not a very good thing. When I teach the beginners, I put in myself as a teacher but I become a greater beginner than those who are learning as beginners. Only then can I teach them. It is just like when you are playing with a child, you have to become a child too. Only then can you get response from the child. How else can you get it?

ON CONTRIBUTION

I do not know, but you people know, what I am doing or not doing. I spent so many years in India and did everything. I wanted to open a real University or College of Music. But I did not get any kind of help. That is why i had to start it outside India. Of course, I put in 40 years of service in India.

GHARANA

My father learned from *Senia Gharana*. It is like a custom or tradition. In the olden times of the rulers, their sons became kings and like that you see, and of course, my father was a disciple of *Senia Gharana* of Mohammad Wazir Khan Sahib, but I am not, because I learned from my father. Therefore, now it has become my *gharana*, my father's *gharana*. The *Allauddin Gharana* of Universal music belongs to the universe. This kind of sound is the language of God. It belongs to the whole universe and, of course, *gharana* is my father's *Allauddin Gharana*. It all comes like that, you see. *Senia Gharana* had Tansen's direct descendants.

Ustad Ali Akbar Khan was a legendary torchbearer of his legendary father's legacy. His passing has left a void in the world of Indian Classical Music that cannot be filled. It was Ustad Allauddin Khan himself who said, "Ali Akbar has a God-gifted genius. His intellect is quite different from the others. Both of Ali Akbar's hands move equally skillfully when he plays. He is absorbed, with all his own brain, mind and heart in his creativity. He has his own creations. His genius is outstanding and unmatchable."

About The Author

Anjana Roy comes from Delhi, India, where she had her early initiation in music under Shri Rebati Ranjan Debnath, her father and guru, who was a disciple of Ustad Allauddin Khan of Maihar. Later she learned from several masters of the art. Anjana earned her Master's in Arts (instrumental music – sitar) from Banasthali Vidyapith of Jaipur, Rajasthan under the guidance of Shri Rameshwar Dayal Verma. She continued her training under Shri Sachin Datta (disciple of Ustad Allauddin Khan) in Delhi. Afterwards, Ms. Roy received the degree of Master of Philosophy (instrumental music – sitar) from the University of New Delhi, under the guidance of Pandit Debu Chaudhuri. She further studied sitar with Pandit Manilal Nag, and later Shri Prasanna Kumar Singh, a disciple of Pandit Manilal Nag. Settled in New York, Ms. Roy has taught sitar music at the Shikshayatan Institution in Queens, New York, and has performed at the Queens Conservatory of Music, Brooklyn Public Library, International House, the Indian Consulate and in many private concerts. Currently Ms. Roy is studying under the tutelage of Shri Parimal M. Sadaphal from Delhi, who is a senior disciple of Pandit Ravi Shankar and one of the foremost sitarists of India. Ms. Roy released a CD of Indian Classical Music on sitar featuring Raga Bageshree in the year 2006.

Anjana Roy Email: sitar@anjanaroy.com Web: http://www.anjanaroy.com Cell: 347.439.3850

CPSIA information can be obtained at www.ICGtesting.com
Printed in the USA
BVOW05s1500190914

367460BV00001B/42/P